Generis
PUBLISHING

# Embedded Linux Based IoT Systems Design, Develop, and Deploy Connected Devices

*Pr Abdellatif Rahmoun*
*Dr. Hamdane Bensenane*

Title: **Embedded Linux Based IoT Systems Design, Develop, and Deploy Connected Devices**

ISBN: 979-8-89966-445-8

Author: Pr Abdellatif Rahmoun, Dr. Hamdane Bensenane

Cover image: https://pixabay.com/

Publisher: Generis Publishing
Online orders: www.generis-publishing.com
Contact email: info@generis-publishing.com

# EMBEDDED LINUX BASED IOT SYSTEMS

## *Design, Develop, and Deploy Connected Devices*

By Professor Abdellatif Rahmoun & Dr Hamdan Bensenane

# Table of Contents

# Chapter 1: Introduction to Embedded Linux IoT Systems

The convergence of embedded systems, Linux operating systems, and Internet of Things (IoT) technologies has fundamentally transformed how we interact with the digital world. This chapter provides a comprehensive introduction to the field of embedded Linux-based IoT systems, establishing the foundational knowledge necessary for understanding the subsequent technical discussions.

## 1.1 The Evolution of Embedded Systems

Embedded systems have evolved dramatically since their inception in the 1960s. Initially designed as simple microcontrollers for specific tasks, modern embedded systems now incorporate powerful processors, extensive memory, and sophisticated operating systems capable of running full-fledged Linux distributions.

### 1.1.1 Historical Perspective

The first embedded systems emerged with the Apollo Guidance Computer in the 1960s, demonstrating that computers could be dedicated to specific tasks within larger systems. The Intel 4004, released in 1971, marked the beginning of the microprocessor era, enabling cost-effective embedded computing. Throughout the 1980s and 1990s, 8-bit and 16-bit microcontrollers dominated the market, with systems typically running bare-metal code or simple real-time operating systems.

The 2000s saw the emergence of 32-bit ARM processors in embedded applications, bringing unprecedented computing power to cost-sensitive devices. The ARM Cortex-A series, introduced in 2005, provided performance comparable to desktop processors while maintaining the power efficiency essential for embedded deployment. This evolution enabled the transition from proprietary RTOS to full Linux systems in embedded contexts.

### 1.1.2 Key Drivers of Evolution

This evolution has been driven by several key factors:

- **Moore's Law Continuation:**The continuous doubling of transistor density has enabled increasingly powerful processors in smaller form factors with reduced power consumption. Modern ARM processors pack billions of transistors into chips smaller than a fingernail.
- **Connectivity Demands:**The need for devices to communicate over networks has necessitated more sophisticated software stacks capable of handling TCP/IP, wireless protocols, and security requirements.
- **User Expectations:**Modern users expect rich interfaces and seamless connectivity from all their devices, driving requirements for graphical displays, touch input, and cloud integration.
- **Cost Reduction:**Mass production and integration have made powerful computing accessible at commodity prices, with complete Linux-capable systems available for under ten dollars.

### 1.1.3 The Linux Revolution in Embedded

The transition from bare-metal programming and proprietary real-time operating systems (RTOS) to full Linux-based systems represents a paradigm shift in embedded development. Linux offers several advantages that have driven its adoption:

The open-source nature eliminates licensing fees, which is critical for high-volume IoT deployments where per-unit costs directly impact profitability. A typical proprietary RTOS might cost $1-5 per unit in royalties; for a million-unit deployment, this represents significant savings when using Linux.

Extensive hardware support means that Linux likely already supports the processor and peripherals in a new design, reducing bring-up time and enabling faster time-to-market. The Linux kernel supports thousands of device drivers out of the box.

## 1.2 Understanding the Internet of Things

The Internet of Things represents a fundamental shift in how we conceptualize connectivity. Rather than viewing the internet as a network of computers, IoT expands this vision to encompass billions of physical devices embedded with sensors, software, and connectivity capabilities.

### 1.2.1 Definition and Scope

The Internet of Things can be defined as a network of physical objects embedded with sensors, software, and connectivity capabilities that enable these objects to collect and exchange data. This definition encompasses a vast range of devices, from simple temperature sensors to complex industrial machinery.

The scope of IoT extends across virtually every industry sector. Consumer IoT includes smart home devices, wearables, and connected vehicles. Industrial IoT (IIoT) encompasses manufacturing equipment, supply chain systems, and infrastructure monitoring. Healthcare IoT includes patient monitors, connected medical devices, and pharmaceutical tracking systems. Smart city IoT covers traffic management, environmental monitoring, and public safety systems.

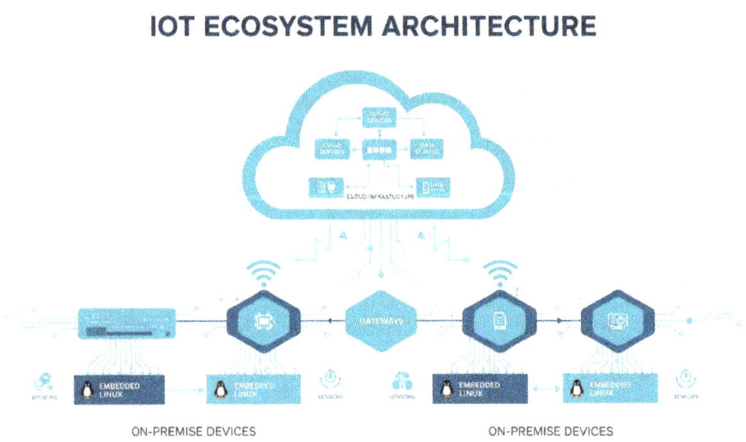


*Figure 1.1: IoT Ecosystem Architecture showing device-to-cloud connectivity*

### 1.2.2 The IoT Architecture Stack

The IoT ecosystem can be conceptualized as a multi-layered architecture comprising several distinct tiers:

0. **Perception Layer:**The physical interface where sensors and actuators interact with the environment. This layer includes temperature sensors, motion detectors, cameras, accelerometers, gyroscopes, pressure sensors, and control mechanisms such as motors, relays, and valves. The perception layer is responsible for converting physical phenomena into digital data and vice versa.
1. **Network Layer:**Responsible for data transmission between devices and the cloud. This encompasses various communication protocols including WiFi, Bluetooth, Zigbee, LoRaWAN, cellular networks, and emerging standards like Thread and Matter. The network layer must handle challenges including intermittent connectivity, bandwidth constraints, and power efficiency.
2. **Processing Layer:**Where data is aggregated, processed, and analyzed. This can occur at the edge (on the device), in fog computing nodes, or in centralized cloud infrastructure. Edge processing reduces latency and bandwidth requirements while enabling autonomous operation during connectivity outages.
3. **Application Layer:**The user-facing interface where insights are presented and control commands are issued. This includes mobile applications, web dashboards, enterprise systems, and APIs for integration with other systems.

### 1.2.3 IoT Market Dynamics

The IoT market has experienced explosive growth over the past decade and shows no signs of slowing. According to industry analysts, the global IoT market is projected to reach over $1.3 trillion by 2027, with billions of connected devices deployed worldwide.

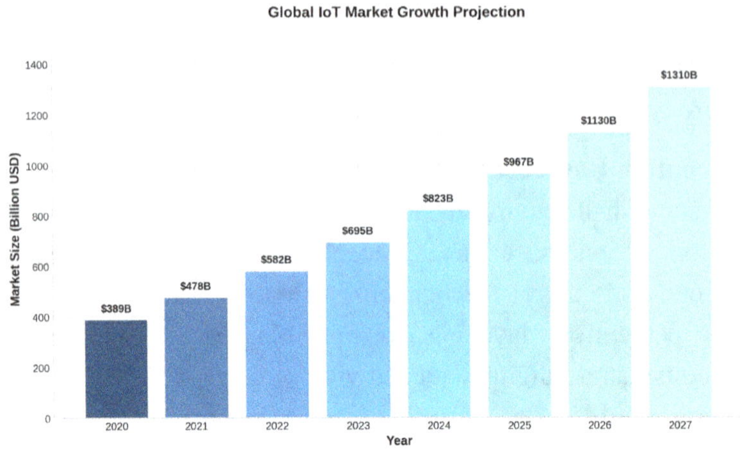


*Figure 1.2: Global IoT Market Growth Projection (2020-2027)*

Several industry verticals are driving this growth:

- **Industrial IoT (IIoT):**Manufacturing facilities are deploying connected sensors for predictive maintenance, quality control, and supply chain optimization. The IIoT market is expected to reach $263 billion by 2027, driven by the need for operational efficiency and reduced downtime.
- **Smart Cities:**Urban infrastructure including traffic management, waste collection, street lighting, and environmental monitoring increasingly relies on IoT networks. Smart city investments are projected to exceed $158 billion by 2025.
- **Healthcare:**Remote patient monitoring, connected medical devices, and pharmaceutical supply chain tracking are transforming healthcare delivery. The healthcare IoT market is growing at over 25% annually.
- **Agriculture:**Precision farming techniques use soil sensors, weather stations, drones, and automated irrigation systems to optimize crop yields while reducing water and fertilizer usage.
- **Smart Home:**Consumer adoption of connected thermostats, security systems, lighting, and appliances continues to accelerate, with over 300 million smart homes expected by 2025.

## 1.3 Why Linux for IoT?

Linux has emerged as the dominant operating system for sophisticated IoT deployments, and this dominance is not accidental. Several key characteristics make Linux particularly well-suited for IoT applications.

### 1.3.1 Open Source Advantages

The open-source nature of Linux provides unparalleled flexibility. Developers can examine, modify, and optimize every aspect of the operating system to meet specific requirements. This transparency is particularly valuable in IoT contexts where devices may have unusual hardware configurations or stringent resource constraints.

Furthermore, the absence of licensing fees reduces the per-unit cost, which is critical for high-volume IoT deployments. Unlike proprietary operating systems that charge per-device royalties, Linux can be deployed at any scale without incremental licensing costs. This economic advantage is substantial: a device shipping one million units annually saves millions of dollars in royalty fees by using Linux instead of a proprietary alternative charging even one dollar per unit.

The open-source model also enables vendor independence. Organizations are not locked into a single supplier for support and maintenance. A vibrant ecosystem of consultants, integrators, and community contributors provides multiple sources of expertise and assistance.

### 1.3.2 Hardware Support and Portability

Linux supports an extraordinarily diverse range of processor architectures, from ARM Cortex-M microcontrollers to high-performance x86_64 processors. This architectural neutrality allows developers to select the optimal hardware platform for their specific application without being constrained by software compatibility.

The device tree mechanism in modern Linux kernels enables clean separation of hardware description from kernel code, facilitating porting to new platforms. When a new processor or board is developed, only the device tree description and potentially a small amount of board-specific code need to be created; the vast majority of the kernel remains unchanged.

Linux also provides extensive driver support for peripherals. The kernel includes thousands of device drivers for network interfaces, storage controllers, sensors, displays, and other components. This driver ecosystem significantly reduces development effort and time-to-market for new devices.

### 1.3.3 Networking and Connectivity

Robust networking support is fundamental to IoT, and Linux excels in this domain. The kernel includes comprehensive implementations of TCP/IP, wireless networking protocols, and emerging IoT-specific protocols such as 6LoWPAN and Thread.

The socket-based networking API provides a consistent interface regardless of the underlying transport mechanism. Application code written for Ethernet can often work with WiFi or cellular connectivity with minimal or no modification. This abstraction simplifies application development and enables portability across different network configurations.

Linux also provides sophisticated network management capabilities including routing, firewalling, network address translation, and traffic shaping. These features enable complex network topologies and enable devices to function as gateways or routers in addition to their primary application functions.

### 1.3.4 Security Features

Security is paramount in IoT deployments, where compromised devices can have serious real-world consequences. Linux provides multiple security mechanisms including discretionary access control, mandatory access control (SELinux, AppArmor), namespaces for isolation, and secure boot capabilities.

The active open-source community ensures rapid identification and patching of vulnerabilities. When security issues are discovered, patches are typically available within days or even hours, compared to the weeks or months that proprietary vendors may require. This responsiveness is critical for maintaining security in the face of evolving threats.

## 1.4 Embedded Linux Ecosystem

The embedded Linux ecosystem encompasses a rich collection of tools, frameworks, and communities that support development and deployment.

### 1.4.1 Build Systems and Distributions

Several build systems simplify the creation of custom Linux distributions for embedded targets. The Yocto Project provides a comprehensive, flexible framework for building complete system images. Buildroot offers a simpler alternative for smaller projects. Commercial distributions like Ubuntu Core and Wind River Linux provide professionally supported options with enterprise features.

### 1.4.2 Development Tools

The GNU toolchain (GCC, binutils, GDB) provides industry-standard compilation and debugging capabilities. Cross-compilation enables building on powerful development hosts for target deployment on resource-constrained devices. Integrated development environments like Eclipse and VS Code provide sophisticated editing, debugging, and profiling capabilities.

### 1.4.3 Community and Support

The Linux kernel mailing lists, Stack Overflow, and numerous specialized forums provide extensive community support. Commercial support is available from vendors including Canonical, Wind River, and MontaVista. Documentation ranges from kernel source code comments to comprehensive books and online resources.

## 1.5 Book Organization and Approach

This book is organized to provide a comprehensive journey through the design, development, and deployment of embedded Linux-based IoT systems. The chapters progress from foundational concepts through advanced topics, with practical examples and case studies throughout.

Chapters 1 through 3 establish the theoretical foundation, covering embedded Linux fundamentals and IoT architecture. Chapters 4 through 7 delve into the technical implementation details of bootloaders, kernel configuration, device drivers, and filesystems. Chapters 8 through 10 address connectivity, security, and cloud integration. Chapters 11 and 12 present real-world case studies and explore emerging trends.

Each chapter includes practical examples, code snippets, architectural diagrams, and hands-on exercises to reinforce theoretical concepts with concrete implementation guidance. The goal is to equip readers with both the understanding and the skills necessary to build production-quality embedded Linux IoT systems.

# Chapter 2: Linux Fundamentals for Embedded Systems

Before diving into the specifics of embedded Linux development, it is essential to establish a solid understanding of Linux fundamentals as they apply to resource-constrained environments. This chapter examines the Linux architecture, kernel components, system organization, and practical considerations for embedded deployment.

## 2.1 Linux Architecture Overview

Linux follows a monolithic kernel architecture with loadable module support. Understanding this architecture is crucial for embedded developers who must optimize system resources and configure kernels for specific hardware platforms.

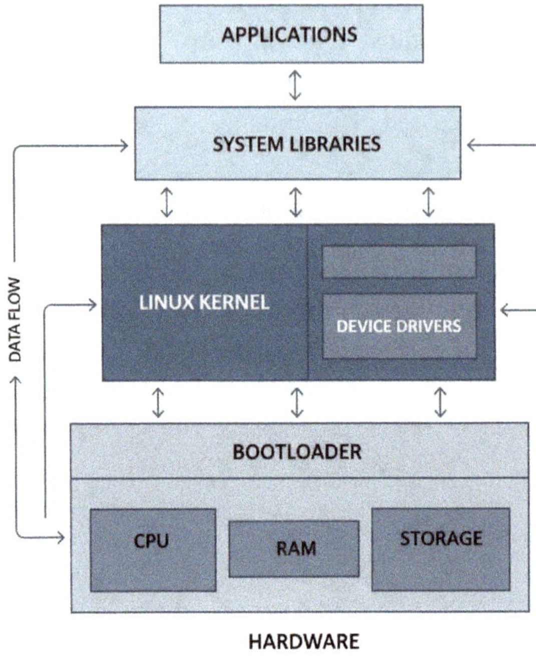


*Figure 2.1: Linux System Architecture showing layered components*

### 2.1.1 Hardware Abstraction Layer

At the foundation lies the hardware abstraction layer, which provides a uniform interface to diverse hardware components. The device tree mechanism, prevalent in ARM-based embedded systems, describes hardware configuration in a structured data format that the kernel parses at boot time. This approach eliminates the need for hardcoded hardware descriptions in kernel source code, facilitating portability across different platforms.

The hardware abstraction layer includes board support packages (BSPs) that provide initialization code, device tree descriptions, and platform-specific drivers. For a new hardware platform, developing a BSP is typically the first step in enabling Linux support. The BSP abstracts platform-specific details, allowing the majority of the kernel to remain unchanged.

### 2.1.2 Kernel Space Components

The Linux kernel operates in privileged processor mode with direct hardware access. Key kernel subsystems include:

- **Process Scheduler:**Manages CPU time allocation among competing processes. The Completely Fair Scheduler (CFS) is the default in modern Linux, providing fair CPU distribution while maintaining good interactive response. For real-time applications, the SCHED_FIFO and SCHED_RR policies provide priority-based scheduling.
- **Memory Management Unit:**Implements virtual memory, translating virtual addresses to physical addresses and managing memory protection. The MMU enables process isolation, shared libraries, and demand paging.
- **Virtual Filesystem Layer:**Provides a unified interface to diverse filesystem implementations. Applications use standard system calls (open, read, write) regardless of the underlying filesystem type.
- **Networking Stack:**Implements TCP/IP and other network protocols. The socket interface provides a consistent API for network programming across different transport mechanisms.
- **Device Driver Framework:**Manages hardware devices through a unified interface. Character devices, block devices, and network devices each have defined interfaces and registration mechanisms.

### 2.1.3 User Space Environment

User space contains applications, libraries, and system services running in unprivileged mode. The system call interface provides the boundary between user space and kernel space, with well-defined entry points for requesting kernel services.

Embedded systems often employ specialized C libraries to reduce memory footprint. The musl libc provides a lightweight, standards-compliant implementation suitable for embedded use. uClibc-ng is another option optimized for size. These libraries can be significantly smaller than the GNU C Library while providing the functionality required by most applications.

## 2.2 The Linux Kernel

The Linux kernel is the core component of any Linux-based system. For embedded developers, understanding kernel configuration, compilation, and customization is essential for creating efficient, purpose-built systems.

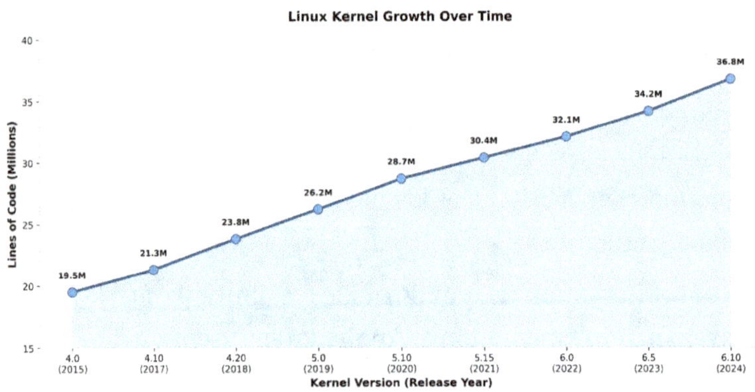


*Figure 2.2: Linux Kernel Growth Over Time (Lines of Code in Millions)*

### 2.2.1 Kernel Versioning and Release Model

Linux kernel development follows a predictable release cycle. New major versions are released approximately every 2-3 months, with version numbers following a semantic format. Version 5.10, for example, indicates major version 5, minor version 10.

Long-Term Support (LTS) kernels are designated every year and maintained for at least two years, with some supported for six years or more.

For embedded systems, LTS kernels are generally preferred as they receive security updates and bug fixes for extended periods, reducing maintenance overhead. The current LTS kernels include versions 5.4, 5.10, 5.15, and 6.1.

### 2.2.2 Kernel Configuration System

The kernel configuration system uses Kconfig files to define available options and their dependencies. Configuration can be managed through various interfaces:

- **make menuconfig:**Ncurses-based graphical interface providing hierarchical navigation and search. This is the most commonly used configuration tool for embedded development.
- **make xconfig:**Qt-based graphical interface with tree view and search capabilities.
- **make gconfig:**GTK-based graphical interface similar to xconfig.
- **make oldconfig:**Updates an existing configuration for a new kernel version, prompting only for new options.
- **make defconfig:**Generates a default configuration based on the architecture.

The resulting configuration is stored in a .config file that controls which features are compiled into the kernel, compiled as modules, or excluded entirely. This file can be saved and reused across builds, enabling reproducible kernel configurations.

### 2.2.3 Kernel Configuration Categories

Key configuration categories for embedded systems include:

- **General Setup:**Kernel compression, initramfs, system configuration options, and build settings.
- **Enable Loadable Module Support:**Whether to support kernel modules or build everything into the kernel.
- **Processor Type and Features:**CPU-specific optimizations, SMP support, and processor features.

- **Power Management:**CPU frequency scaling, suspend/resume, and runtime power management options.
- **Bus Support:**PCI, PCI Express, and other bus configurations.
- **Networking Support:**Network protocols, wireless, and networking options.
- **Device Drivers:**The largest category, containing drivers for all supported hardware types.
- **File Systems:**Support for various filesystem types including ext4, SquashFS, and UBIFS.

## 2.3 Memory Management in Embedded Linux

Memory management is particularly critical in embedded systems where RAM is often a scarce resource. Linux employs sophisticated memory management techniques that must be understood and appropriately configured for embedded deployments.

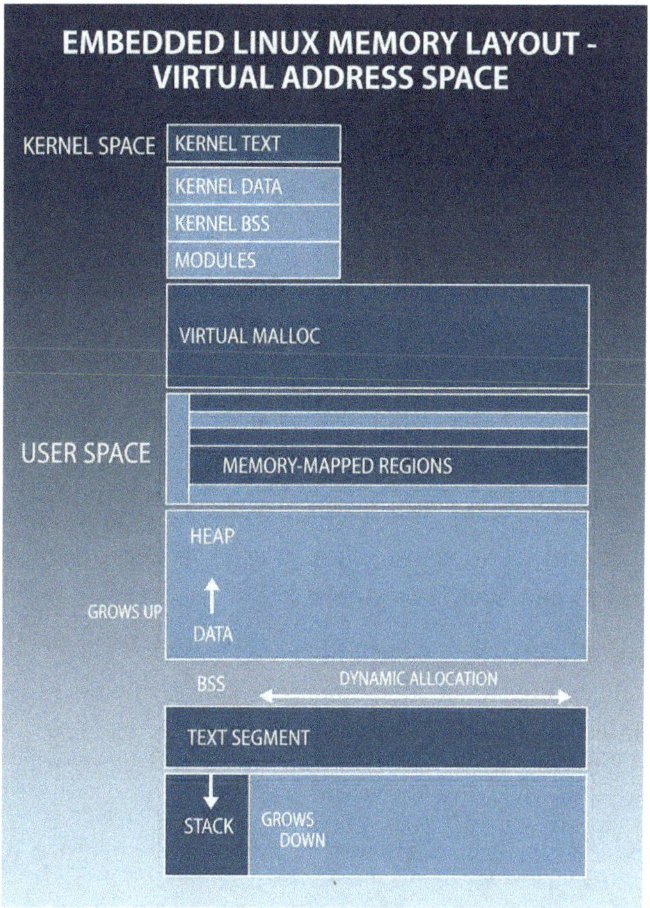


*Figure 2.3: Linux Virtual Memory Layout in Embedded Systems*

### 2.3.1 Virtual Memory Architecture

Linux implements a virtual memory system where each process operates in its own address space, isolated from other processes. The Memory Management Unit (MMU) hardware translates virtual addresses to physical addresses, enabling memory protection and efficient memory utilization.

In typical 32-bit ARM systems, the virtual address space is divided with kernel space occupying the upper 1GB (0xC0000000 to 0xFFFFFFFF) and user space occupying the lower 3GB (0x00000000 to 0xBFFFFFFF).

This split can be adjusted at kernel configuration time, with some systems using a 2GB/2GB split for applications requiring larger address spaces.

### 2.3.2 Memory Allocation Strategies

The kernel provides multiple memory allocation interfaces with different characteristics:

- **kmalloc:**Allocates physically contiguous memory from the kernel's slab allocator. Required for DMA operations. Limited by physical memory fragmentation.
- **vmalloc:**Allocates virtually contiguous but potentially physically fragmented memory. Suitable for larger allocations where physical contiguity is not required.
- **page allocator:**Allocates entire pages of memory. Used for large allocations and memory-mapped I/O.

Understanding these interfaces is essential for device driver development, as improper allocation can lead to memory fragmentation, allocation failures, or performance degradation.

### 2.3.3 Memory Optimization Techniques

Embedded systems often require aggressive memory optimization. Techniques include:

- **Kernel Size Reduction:**Remove unnecessary drivers, filesystems, and features from the kernel configuration.
- **Compressed Kernel:**Use kernel compression (gzip, LZO, LZ4) to reduce storage requirements at the cost of decompression time.
- **Minimal Root Filesystem:**Use BusyBox or custom minimal user space instead of full distributions.
- **Read-Only Root:**Mount the root filesystem read-only with tmpfs overlays for writable data.

## 2.4 Process Management and Scheduling

Linux implements a preemptive multitasking scheduler that allocates CPU time among competing processes. Understanding scheduling behavior is important for meeting application timing requirements.

### 2.4.1 The Linux Scheduler

The Completely Fair Scheduler (CFS) is the default scheduler in modern Linux kernels. It uses a red-black tree data structure to track runnable processes and allocates CPU time proportionally to process priorities. CFS provides good overall throughput while maintaining reasonable interactive response.

For applications requiring more deterministic behavior, Linux provides real-time scheduling policies. SCHED_FIFO provides first-in-first-out scheduling with priority preemption. SCHED_RR provides round-robin scheduling within priority levels. Real-time processes can starve normal processes, so care must be taken to prevent system lockup.

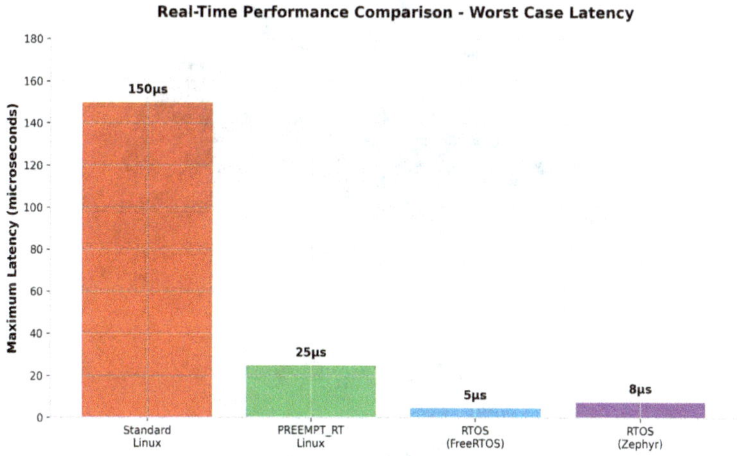


*Figure 2.4: Real-Time Performance Comparison - Worst Case Latency*

### 2.4.2 Real-Time Linux

Standard Linux is not a hard real-time operating system, but the PREEMPT_RT patch set provides real-time capabilities suitable for many

IoT applications. This patch set makes most kernel code preemptible and introduces priority inheritance to avoid priority inversion.

Key PREEMPT_RT features include threaded interrupt handlers that run as kernel threads, spinlock conversion to mutexes with priority inheritance, and high-resolution timers for precise timing. With PREEMPT_RT, Linux can achieve worst-case latencies in the tens of microseconds, sufficient for many control and signal processing applications.

## 2.5 Embedded Linux Distributions

Unlike desktop Linux, embedded systems typically use specialized distributions or build systems designed for cross-compilation and minimal resource consumption.

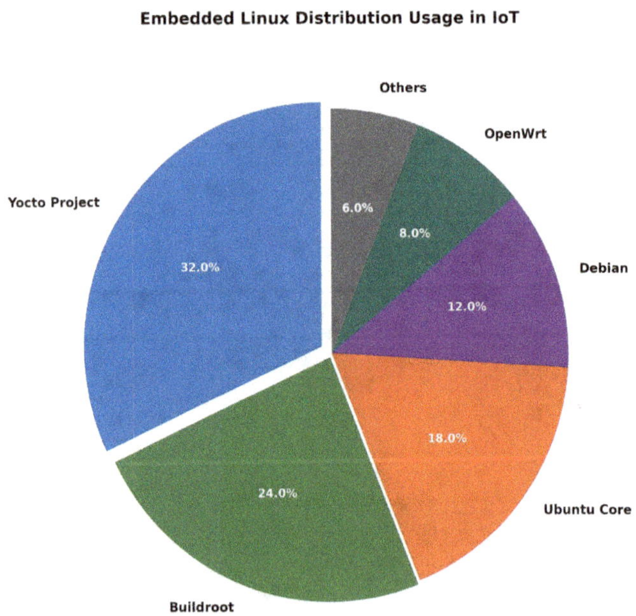


*Figure 2.5: Embedded Linux Distribution Usage in IoT Applications*

## 2.5.1 Yocto Project

The Yocto Project provides a comprehensive build system for creating custom Linux distributions. It uses a metadata structure with recipes describing how to build individual packages, and layers providing hardware support and feature sets.

Yocto enables reproducible builds and extensive customization but has a steep learning curve. The layer mechanism allows separation of concerns, with hardware-specific code in BSP layers, application code in custom layers, and common functionality in shared layers.

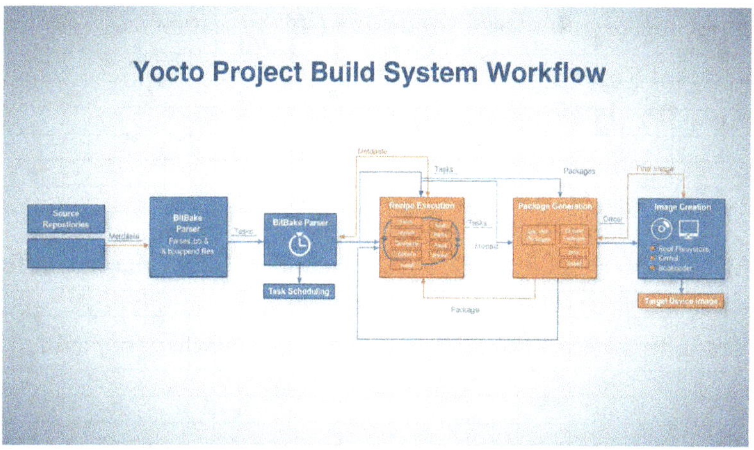


*Figure 2.6: Yocto Project Build System Workflow*

## 2.5.2 Buildroot

Buildroot offers a simpler alternative to Yocto, using makefiles and Kconfig for configuration. It is well-suited for smaller projects requiring a quick path to a working system. While less flexible than Yocto, Buildroot's simplicity makes it attractive for straightforward embedded deployments.

Buildroot generates a root filesystem image, kernel, and bootloader in a single build process. It supports a wide range of target architectures and provides package management for common software components.

### 2.5.3 Commercial Distributions

Several vendors provide commercial embedded Linux distributions with professional support:

- **Ubuntu Core:**Based on Ubuntu Server, offering snap-based application packaging and over-the-air updates. Strong security model with application confinement.
- **Wind River Linux:**Enterprise-focused distribution with extensive testing, certification, and long-term support options.
- **MontaVista Carrier Grade Edition:**Targets high-reliability applications with carrier-grade availability features.
- **Red Hat Enterprise Linux for Edge:**Brings enterprise Linux features to edge deployments with centralized management.

## 2.6 ARM Architecture for Embedded

ARM processors dominate the embedded Linux market, offering an excellent balance of performance, power efficiency, and cost. Understanding ARM architecture is essential for embedded Linux developers.

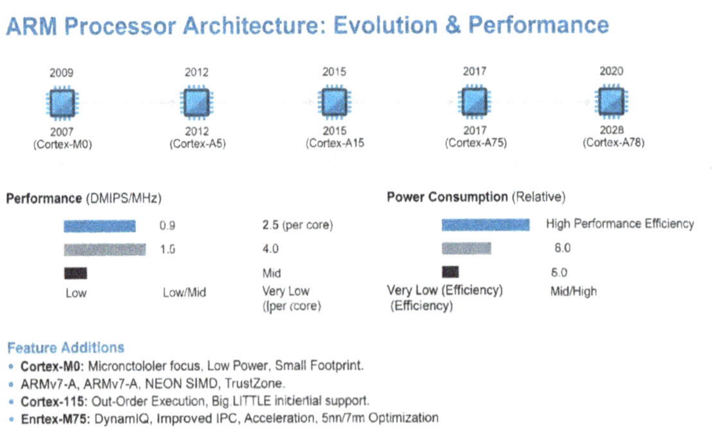


*Figure 2.7: ARM Processor Architecture Evolution and Performance*

### 2.6.1 ARM Processor Families

ARM offers several processor families targeting different application spaces:

- **Cortex-A Series:**Application processors capable of running full Linux. Includes single-core to octa-core configurations with frequencies exceeding 2 GHz.
- **Cortex-R Series:**Real-time processors for applications requiring deterministic response. Limited Linux support due to memory protection constraints.
- **Cortex-M Series:**Microcontrollers typically running RTOS or bare-metal code. Cortex-M4 and above can run limited Linux variants.

### 2.6.2 ARM System Architecture

ARM systems typically include the processor core, interrupt controller (GIC), timer, and debug interface. SoC vendors add memory controllers, peripheral interfaces, and specialized accelerators. The ARM TrustZone technology provides hardware-based security isolation between secure and normal worlds.

The device tree is the standard mechanism for describing ARM hardware to the kernel. Device tree source files (.dts) are compiled to binary blobs (.dtb) that the kernel parses at boot to discover available hardware.

# Chapter 3: IoT Architecture and Protocols

The architecture of IoT systems presents unique challenges that differentiate them from traditional networked applications. This chapter examines the architectural patterns, communication protocols, and design considerations essential for building scalable and reliable IoT deployments.

## 3.1 IoT Architectural Patterns

IoT systems can be organized according to several architectural patterns, each with distinct advantages and trade-offs. The selection of an appropriate pattern depends on factors including scale, latency requirements, connectivity constraints, and processing distribution.

### 3.1.1 Device-to-Cloud Architecture

The simplest IoT architecture connects devices directly to cloud services. This pattern is straightforward to implement and leverages the extensive computational resources of cloud platforms. However, it can introduce latency issues, creates dependency on internet connectivity, and may generate substantial data transfer costs for high-frequency sensor data.

Device-to-cloud architectures work well for applications with infrequent data transmission, tolerance for cloud latency, and reliable internet connectivity. Simple monitoring applications, periodic telemetry, and devices with sufficient processing power for TLS encryption are good candidates for this pattern.

### 3.1.2 Device-to-Gateway Architecture

In this pattern, edge devices communicate through a local gateway that aggregates data and manages cloud connectivity. The gateway can perform local processing, filtering, and protocol translation. This architecture reduces bandwidth requirements, enables local autonomy when cloud connectivity is unavailable, and can improve security by limiting direct internet exposure of edge devices.

Gateway architectures are appropriate for sensor networks with many nodes, applications requiring local processing, and deployments with intermittent connectivity. The gateway can run more powerful software stacks than individual sensors, enabling complex data processing and sophisticated security mechanisms.

### 3.1.3 Fog Computing Architecture

Fog computing extends the gateway concept by distributing computational resources throughout the network hierarchy. Processing can occur at the edge, in intermediate fog nodes, or in the cloud, depending on latency requirements, data volume, and privacy considerations.

This architecture is particularly valuable for applications requiring real-time response or handling sensitive data. Industrial control systems, autonomous vehicles, and video analytics applications benefit from fog computing's distributed processing capabilities.

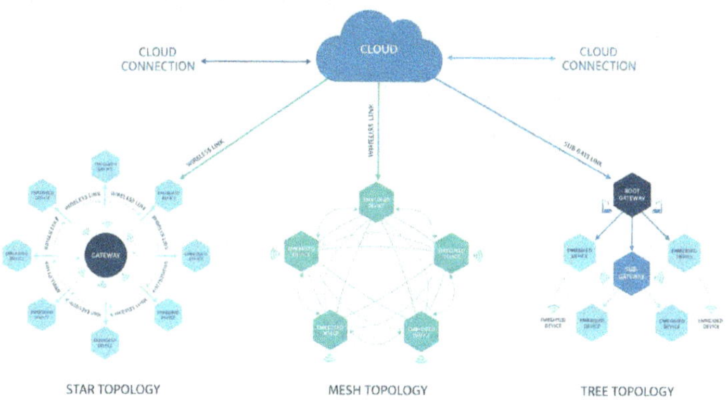


*Figure 3.1: IoT Network Topologies - Star, Mesh, and Tree Configurations*

## 3.2 Communication Protocols for IoT

IoT communication spans multiple protocol layers, from physical radio technologies to application-layer messaging protocols. Understanding the protocol stack is essential for designing efficient and interoperable systems.

### 3.2.1 Physical and Link Layer Protocols

The choice of physical layer technology significantly impacts device power consumption, range, and data rate. Common options include:

- **WiFi (802.11):**High bandwidth (up to gigabits per second) and widespread infrastructure, but relatively high power consumption (hundreds of milliwatts). Suitable for powered devices requiring significant data throughput.
- **Bluetooth Low Energy (BLE):**Ultra-low power consumption (microamps in sleep) ideal for battery-operated devices. Limited range (typically 10-100 meters) and bandwidth constrain applications.
- **Zigbee and Z-Wave:**Mesh networking protocols designed for home automation with good range extension through relay nodes. Low power consumption suitable for battery-operated sensors.
- **LoRaWAN:**Long-range (kilometers), low-power protocol for wide-area IoT deployments. Very low data rates (hundreds of bits per second) suitable for infrequent sensor transmissions.
- **Cellular (NB-IoT, LTE-M):**Wide-area coverage using existing cellular infrastructure. Higher power consumption but excellent coverage and reliability. NB-IoT is optimized for low data rate, infrequent transmission applications.

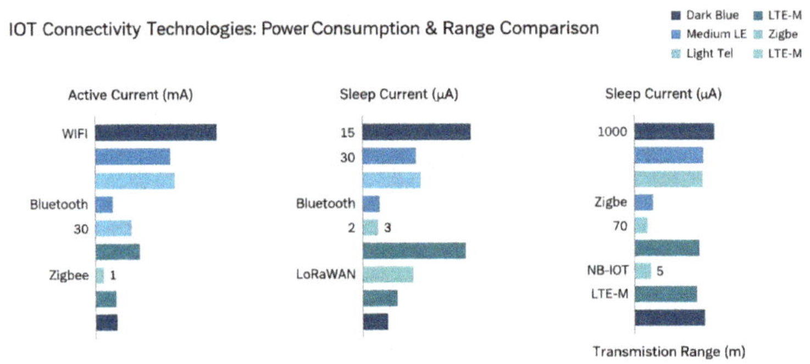


*Figure 3.2: IoT Connectivity Technologies - Power Consumption and Range Comparison*

### 3.2.2 Network Layer: IPv6 and 6LoWPAN

The transition to IPv6 is essential for IoT scalability, given the exhaustion of IPv4 address space. IPv6 provides approximately 3.4 x 10^38 addresses, sufficient to assign unique addresses to every conceivable IoT device.

6LoWPAN (IPv6 over Low-Power Wireless Personal Area Networks) adapts IPv6 for constrained devices by providing header compression and fragmentation support. This enables direct IP connectivity for even the most resource-constrained sensors, allowing end-to-end IP communication from sensor to cloud.

### 3.2.3 Transport Layer Considerations

TCP provides reliable, ordered delivery but introduces overhead that may be excessive for constrained devices. The three-way handshake, acknowledgment packets, and congestion control add latency and bandwidth overhead.

UDP offers lower overhead but requires application-level reliability mechanisms if needed. For many IoT applications, UDP-based protocols with application-level acknowledgment are preferred for efficiency. CoAP, for example, runs over UDP with optional reliability mechanisms.

## 3.3 Application Layer Protocols

Several application-layer protocols have been developed specifically for IoT communication, each optimized for different use cases and constraints.

### 3.3.1 MQTT (Message Queuing Telemetry Transport)

MQTT has emerged as the dominant messaging protocol for IoT. Developed by IBM in the late 1990s for oil pipeline monitoring, MQTT was designed from the ground up for constrained devices and unreliable networks.

MQTT uses a publish-subscribe model with a broker mediating communication between clients. Clients publish messages to topics and subscribe to topics to receive messages. This decoupling of sender and receiver enables flexible, scalable architectures.

Key characteristics include:

- **Lightweight Header:**Minimal protocol overhead with a fixed 2-byte header, making it efficient for low-bandwidth networks.
- **Quality of Service Levels:**Three QoS levels (0: at most once, 1: at least once, 2: exactly once) allow trade-offs between reliability and overhead.
- **Last Will and Testament:**Clients can register messages to be sent if they disconnect unexpectedly, enabling rapid failure detection.
- **Retained Messages:**Brokers can retain the last message on a topic for new subscribers, ensuring late-joining clients receive current state.

MQTT is ideal for telemetry applications, command-and-control scenarios, and any situation requiring efficient, bidirectional communication between devices and backend systems.

### 3.3.2 CoAP (Constrained Application Protocol)

CoAP is designed specifically for constrained devices and networks, providing a RESTful interface similar to HTTP but with dramatically reduced overhead. CoAP uses UDP as its transport, supports multicast, and includes built-in discovery mechanisms.

CoAP messages map directly to HTTP methods (GET, POST, PUT, DELETE), making it familiar to web developers. The binary header format is parseable by constrained devices, and the protocol supports both confirmable (reliable) and non-confirmable (unreliable) messages.

It is particularly well-suited for resource-constrained environments where HTTP would be impractical. CoAP is often used in conjunction with 6LoWPAN for IP-based sensor networks.

### 3.3.3 HTTP/2 and WebSocket

While HTTP/1.1 is generally too heavyweight for constrained IoT devices, HTTP/2's header compression and multiplexing make it more suitable for some applications. HTTP/2's binary framing reduces overhead, and server push can proactively send data to clients.

WebSocket provides full-duplex communication over a single TCP connection, enabling real-time bidirectional data flow. After an initial HTTP handshake, the connection upgrades to WebSocket, allowing low-latency messaging in both directions.

These protocols are most appropriate for gateways or more capable edge devices rather than deeply embedded sensors. They integrate well with existing web infrastructure and development tools.

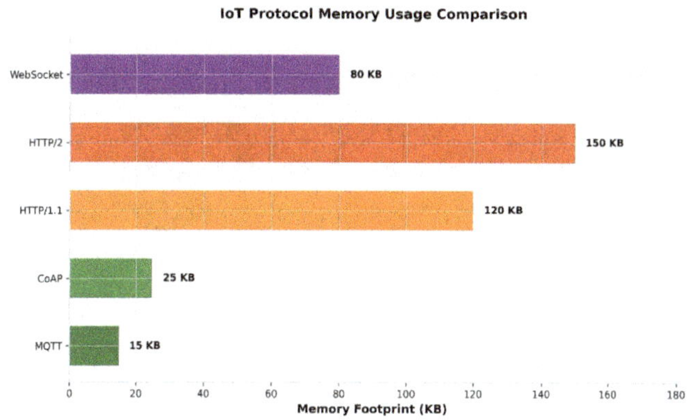


*Figure 3.3: IoT Protocol Memory Usage Comparison*

## 3.4 Data Serialization Formats

Efficient data serialization is critical for bandwidth-constrained IoT networks. Several formats offer different trade-offs between human readability and machine efficiency.

### 3.4.1 JSON (JavaScript Object Notation)

JSON provides human-readable, self-describing data representation that is easy to debug and work with. Its widespread adoption means extensive tooling support in virtually every programming language.

However, its text-based nature and verbose syntax result in larger message sizes compared to binary formats. JSON is most appropriate for gateway-to-cloud communication where bandwidth is less constrained, or for development and debugging scenarios where human readability is valuable.

### 3.4.2 CBOR (Concise Binary Object Representation)

CBOR provides a binary representation that maintains JSON's data model while significantly reducing size. It is standardized in RFC 7049 and is increasingly adopted for constrained IoT communication.

CBOR can represent the same data structures as JSON in roughly 50-70% less space. It supports data types not available in JSON, including binary data and floating-point numbers. The format is designed to be parseable by constrained devices with minimal code footprint.

### 3.4.3 Protocol Buffers

Google's Protocol Buffers offer a schema-based binary serialization with excellent size efficiency and fast parsing. The need for schema definition and code generation adds complexity but provides strong typing and versioning capabilities.

Protocol Buffers are well-suited for internal system communication where both sender and receiver can share schema definitions. The compact binary format and efficient parsing make them ideal for high-throughput applications.

## 3.5 Device Management and OTA Updates

Managing fleets of IoT devices presents significant operational challenges. Device management encompasses provisioning, configuration, monitoring, and software updates across potentially thousands or millions of deployed devices.

### 3.5.1 Device Provisioning

Secure device provisioning establishes the identity and credentials necessary for devices to authenticate with cloud services. Common approaches include:

- **Factory Provisioning:**Unique certificates or keys are programmed during device manufacturing. Provides strong security but requires secure manufacturing processes.
- **Just-in-Time Provisioning:**Devices use device-specific tokens to obtain certificates at first connection. Simplifies manufacturing but requires secure token handling.
- **Certificate Enrollment Protocols:**EST (Enrollment over Secure Transport) and SCEP (Simple Certificate Enrollment Protocol) automate certificate issuance.

Security of the provisioning process is critical, as compromised provisioning can undermine the entire security architecture.

### 3.5.2 Over-the-Air (OTA) Updates

OTA update capability is essential for maintaining device security and functionality throughout the product lifecycle. A robust OTA system must handle:

- **Interrupted Updates:**Power loss or connectivity failure during update must not brick the device.
- **Integrity Verification:**Cryptographic signatures verify that updates are authentic and unmodified.
- **Rollback Capability:**Failed updates can be reverted to the previous working version.
- **Bandwidth Management:**Large updates may need to be delivered in chunks or during off-peak hours.

The update mechanism itself must be secure to prevent malicious firmware installation. Secure boot ensures that only properly signed firmware can execute.

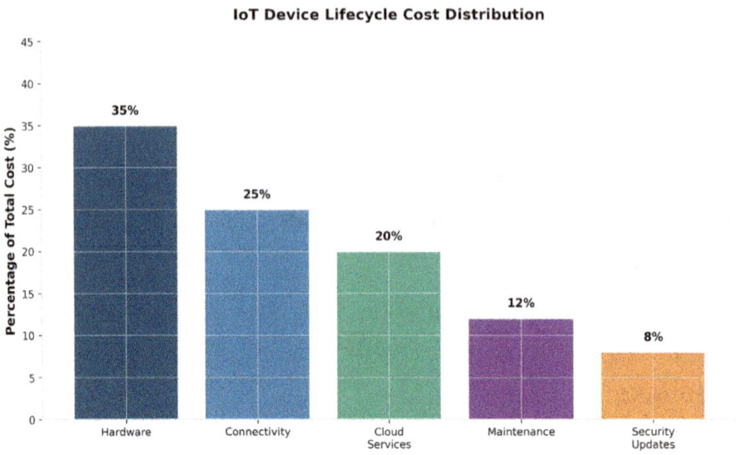


*Figure 3.4: IoT Device Lifecycle Cost Distribution*

# Chapter 4: Bootloaders and Boot Process

The boot process is the critical sequence that transforms a powered-off piece of hardware into a running Linux system. Understanding this process is essential for embedded developers who must configure, customize, and troubleshoot system startup. This chapter examines the boot sequence in detail, with particular focus on the U-Boot bootloader widely used in embedded Linux systems.

## 4.1 The Boot Sequence

The Linux boot process proceeds through several distinct stages, each responsible for initializing specific aspects of the system.

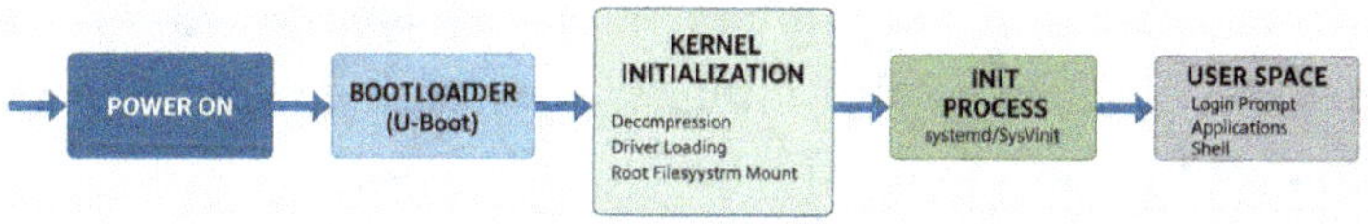


*Figure 4.1: Linux Boot Process Sequence*

### 4.1.1 Power-On and Boot ROM

When power is applied, the processor begins execution at a reset vector defined by the architecture. This address typically points to internal Boot ROM code that performs initial hardware initialization. The Boot ROM is mask-programmed during chip manufacturing and cannot be modified.

The Boot ROM's primary responsibilities include initializing the memory controller to enable access to external DRAM, configuring essential peripherals such as clocks and power management, and locating the next stage bootloader from available boot sources.

Boot ROMs typically support multiple boot sources, selected through strap pins or eFuse configuration. Common boot sources include NAND flash, eMMC, SD card, SPI flash, and network boot via Ethernet. The Boot ROM attempts each configured source in order until a valid bootloader is found.

### 4.1.2 First Stage Bootloader

The first stage bootloader, often called SPL (Secondary Program Loader) in U-Boot terminology, is a minimal bootloader whose sole purpose is to initialize DRAM and load the full bootloader. Due to size constraints in the Boot ROM's load location, this stage is kept as small as possible.

The SPL typically runs from SRAM before main memory is available. It performs minimal hardware initialization, sets up the DRAM controller, and then loads the full U-Boot image from storage into DRAM. Once loaded, control transfers to the full bootloader.

### 4.1.3 Second Stage Bootloader (U-Boot)

The full bootloader provides the interactive environment and boot logic for loading the Linux kernel. U-Boot is the de facto standard bootloader for embedded Linux, supporting hundreds of different boards and processors.

U-Boot provides commands for examining and modifying memory, loading images from various sources (NAND, SD, network), and controlling the boot process. It can be interrupted during the boot delay to provide an interactive command prompt for debugging and recovery.

### 4.1.4 Linux Kernel Initialization

Once loaded, the Linux kernel decompresses itself (if compressed), initializes kernel subsystems, mounts the root filesystem, and starts the init process. The kernel command line parameters passed by the bootloader control many aspects of kernel behavior.

Key kernel command line parameters include console= for specifying the serial console, root= for identifying the root filesystem device, and rootfstype= for specifying the root filesystem type. Additional parameters control debugging, memory configuration, and driver behavior.

## 4.2 U-Boot Deep Dive

U-Boot (Universal Boot Loader) is the most widely used bootloader in embedded Linux systems. Its flexibility, extensive hardware support, and active development community make it the preferred choice for most embedded projects.

### 4.2.1 U-Boot Architecture

U-Boot is organized into several functional components. The command subsystem provides interactive and scripted control through a rich set of commands. The driver framework abstracts hardware access for storage, networking, and peripherals. The image handling code understands various Linux image formats and boot protocols. Board-specific code provides initialization for particular hardware platforms.

U-Boot's modular design allows selective inclusion of features based on target requirements. This configurability is essential for resource-constrained systems where unnecessary features consume valuable storage space.

### 4.2.2 U-Boot Configuration

U-Boot uses a Kconfig-based configuration system similar to the Linux kernel. Configuration options control which drivers, commands, and features are included in the build.

Board-specific configurations are defined in defconfig files that set appropriate defaults for particular hardware platforms. These configurations specify the processor architecture, board-specific initialization, available commands, and driver selection.

Key configuration areas include:

- **Architecture Selection:**Target CPU architecture and specific processor variant.
- **Board Support:**Specific board initialization and hardware configuration.
- **Command Set:**Which U-Boot commands are included in the build.
- **Drivers:**Storage, network, and peripheral drivers for the target hardware.
- **Boot Media Support:**NAND, NOR, eMMC, SD card, network boot capabilities.

### 4.2.3 U-Boot Environment

The U-Boot environment stores configuration variables that control boot behavior. Environment variables can specify the kernel image location, kernel command line arguments, network configuration, and custom boot scripts.

The environment is typically stored in persistent storage such as flash memory or EEPROM, allowing configuration to survive power cycles. The environment can be modified from the U-Boot command line and saved to persistent storage.

Important environment variables include:

- **bootcmd:**The command or script that U-Boot executes automatically after the boot delay.
- **bootargs:**Arguments passed to the Linux kernel as the command line.
- **bootdelay:**Seconds to wait for user interruption before automatic boot.
- **ipaddr/serverip:**Network configuration for TFTP boot.

- **loadaddr:**Default memory address for loading images.

## 4.3 Boot Source Options

Embedded systems can boot from various storage media, each with distinct characteristics affecting reliability, performance, and system design.

### 4.3.1 NAND Flash

NAND flash provides high-density, cost-effective storage but requires bad block management and wear leveling. Raw NAND interfaces directly to the processor memory bus, requiring the bootloader to handle ECC (Error Correcting Code) and bad block management.

NAND flash characteristics include block-based erase operations, limited erase cycles per block (typically 100,000 for SLC, 3,000 for MLC), and potential bad blocks from manufacturing. The bootloader must handle these complexities to ensure reliable boot.

### 4.3.2 eMMC

eMMC (embedded MultiMediaCard) combines NAND flash with an integrated controller in a standardized package. The controller handles bad block management, wear leveling, and ECC, presenting a simple block device interface to the host.

eMMC is widely used in consumer electronics and provides a good balance of cost, capacity, and reliability. The standardized interface simplifies software design, and the integrated controller offloads complexity from the host processor.

### 4.3.3 SD and microSD Cards

SD cards offer removable storage that simplifies development and field updates. They use a similar interface to eMMC and can be booted directly by many processors.

However, SD cards vary widely in quality and performance. Consumer-grade cards may not be suitable for industrial applications requiring high reliability. Industrial-grade SD cards offer better reliability, wider temperature ranges, and more predictable performance.

### 4.3.4 Network Boot

Network booting via TFTP is invaluable during development, allowing rapid iteration without flashing storage. Production systems may also use network boot for diskless operation or centralized management.

PXE (Preboot Execution Environment) and U-Boot's network stack enable loading kernel and filesystem images from network servers. Network boot requires DHCP for IP configuration and TFTP for file transfer.

## 4.4 Boot Time Optimization

Boot time is critical for many IoT applications, particularly battery-powered devices that must quickly perform their function and return to sleep. Optimizing boot time requires analysis and optimization at each stage of the boot process.

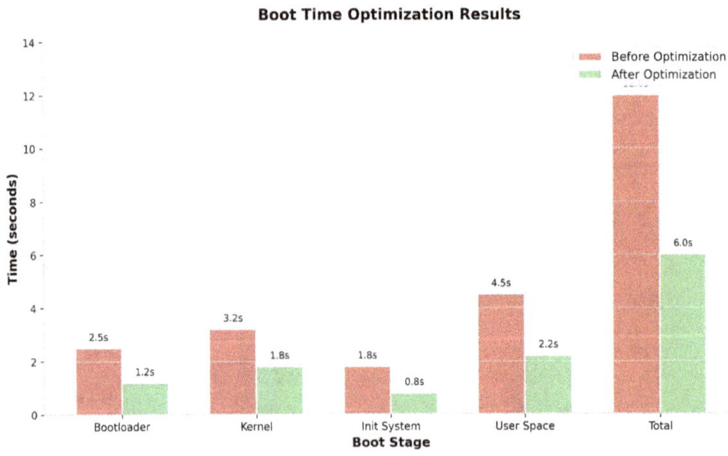


*Figure 4.2: Boot Time Optimization Results by Stage*

### 4.4.1 Bootloader Optimization

U-Boot boot time can be reduced through several techniques:

- **Disable Unnecessary Features:**Remove unused drivers and commands from the U-Boot configuration.
- **Optimize Boot Script:**Streamline the bootcmd script to eliminate unnecessary delays and operations.
- **Use Falcon Mode:**After initial setup, bypass U-Boot entirely and boot directly to Linux.
- **Reduce Console Output:**Disable or minimize boot messages to save serial output time.
- **Zero Boot Delay:**Set bootdelay to 0 for production systems where interactive boot is not needed.

### 4.4.2 Kernel Optimization

Kernel boot time is primarily determined by driver initialization. Optimization techniques include:

- **Compile Drivers Built-in:**Avoid module loading overhead by compiling essential drivers into the kernel.
- **Remove Unnecessary Drivers:**Eliminate drivers for hardware not present in the system.
- **Deferred Probe:**Use deferred probe to parallelize initialization of devices with dependencies.
- **initcall_debug:**Use this option to identify which drivers consume the most boot time.

### 4.4.3 Init System Optimization

The init system starts user-space services and applications. systemd provides extensive parallelization and dependency management, but its overhead may be excessive for simple systems.

Alternative init systems like BusyBox init or custom C-based init programs can significantly reduce startup time for minimal systems. These lightweight alternatives start only essential services and avoid the complexity of full systemd initialization.

# Chapter 5: Linux Kernel Configuration and Compilation

The Linux kernel is the foundation of any embedded Linux system. Configuring and compiling a kernel optimized for specific hardware and application requirements is a fundamental skill for embedded developers. This chapter provides comprehensive guidance on kernel configuration, compilation, and deployment for embedded systems.

## 5.1 Kernel Source and Version Selection

Selecting the appropriate kernel version is a critical decision that affects system stability, hardware support, security, and maintenance requirements.

### 5.1.1 Mainline vs. Vendor Kernels

Mainline Linux kernels from kernel.org represent the official kernel development. They provide the most up-to-date features and broad hardware support but may lack optimizations and drivers for specific SoCs (System on Chip).

Vendor kernels, provided by silicon manufacturers, include hardware-specific drivers and optimizations but may lag behind mainline and include proprietary code. These kernels are often necessary during initial hardware bring-up when mainline support is incomplete.

The ideal approach is to use vendor kernels during initial development for hardware enablement, then migrate to mainline or vendor kernels with minimal patches for production. The Linux kernel's stable release process and long-term support (LTS) versions provide a balance between stability and maintenance.

### 5.1.2 LTS Kernel Strategy

For production embedded systems, LTS kernels are strongly recommended. These kernels receive bug fixes and security updates for several years, reducing maintenance overhead.

The current LTS kernels and their projected support lifetimes should be evaluated when planning product lifecycles. A product with a 10-year expected lifetime may require planning for multiple kernel updates during its deployment.

## 5.2 Kernel Configuration

Kernel configuration determines which features, drivers, and subsystems are included in the build. Proper configuration is essential for creating a kernel that supports the target hardware while minimizing resource consumption.

### 5.2.1 Configuration Methods

Several interfaces are available for kernel configuration:

- **make config:**Text-based interface that prompts for each option sequentially. Tedious but works in any environment.
- **make menuconfig:**Ncurses-based graphical interface. The most commonly used configuration tool, providing hierarchical navigation and search capabilities.
- **make xconfig:**Qt-based graphical interface with tree view and search. Requires X11 or Wayland display.
- **make gconfig:**GTK-based graphical interface similar to xconfig.
- **make oldconfig:**Updates an existing configuration for a new kernel version, prompting only for new options.
- **make defconfig:**Generates a default configuration based on the architecture.

### 5.2.2 Configuration File Structure

The kernel configuration is stored in a .config file in the kernel source root. This file contains lines in the form CONFIG_OPTION=value, where value can be y (built-in), m (module), or n (disabled).

The configuration file can be manually edited, though using the configuration tools is recommended to maintain consistency and dependency satisfaction. The tools handle dependencies between options, ensuring that enabling a feature automatically enables its prerequisites.

### 5.2.3 Key Configuration Categories

Kernel configuration options are organized into categories. For embedded systems, particular attention should be paid to:

- **General Setup:**Kernel compression, initramfs, system configuration options, and build settings.
- **Processor Type and Features:**CPU-specific optimizations, SMP support, and processor features.
- **Power Management:**CPU frequency scaling, suspend/resume, and runtime power management options.
- **Networking Support:**Network protocols, wireless, and networking options.
- **Device Drivers:**The largest category, containing drivers for all supported hardware types.
- **File Systems:**Support for various filesystem types including ext4, SquashFS, and UBIFS.

## 5.3 Kernel Compilation

Compiling the kernel for an embedded target requires a cross-compilation toolchain, as the build typically occurs on a more powerful development host rather than the target device.

### 5.3.1 Cross-Compilation Setup

Cross-compilation requires specifying the target architecture and toolchain prefix. This is done through environment variables or make parameters:

ARCH=arm specifies the target architecture. CROSS_COMPILE=arm-linux-gnueabihf- specifies the toolchain prefix. These can be set as environment variables or passed to make on each invocation.

### 5.3.2 Build Process

The kernel build process involves several stages:

4. **Configuration:**Establish the kernel configuration using one of the configuration methods.
5. **Compilation:**Run make to compile the kernel, modules, and device tree blobs.
6. **Module Installation:**Install kernel modules to a staging directory with make modules_install.
7. **Image Creation:**The kernel image (zImage, uImage, etc.) is created in arch/$ARCH/boot/.
8. **Device Tree Compilation:**Device tree source files are compiled into binary blobs (.dtb files).

### 5.3.3 Kernel Image Formats

Different bootloaders and platforms require different kernel image formats:

- **zImage:**Self-extracting compressed kernel image for ARM. Decompresses and boots in one step.
- **uImage:**U-Boot wrapped image with header containing load address and checksum.
- **Image:**Uncompressed kernel image, rarely used due to size.

- **fitImage:**Flattened Image Tree, supporting multiple images and configurations.

## 5.4 Device Tree

The device tree is a data structure that describes hardware configuration to the kernel. It enables a single kernel binary to support multiple hardware platforms by separating hardware description from kernel code.

### 5.4.1 Device Tree Structure

Device tree source files (.dts) use a hierarchical structure of nodes and properties. Each node represents a device or hardware component, with properties describing its characteristics.

The device tree compiler (dtc) converts source files to binary blobs (.dtb) that the kernel parses at boot. A typical device tree includes nodes for the CPU, memory, buses, and peripherals. Properties specify register addresses, interrupt numbers, clock sources, and other hardware-specific information.

### 5.4.2 Device Tree Overlays

Device tree overlays allow runtime modification of the device tree, enabling support for pluggable hardware without modifying the base device tree. This is particularly useful for expansion boards and hardware variants.

The overlay mechanism is widely used in platforms like Raspberry Pi and BeagleBone. Overlays are compiled separately and applied to the base device tree at boot time, adding or modifying nodes as needed.

## 5.5 Kernel Modules

Kernel modules provide a mechanism for dynamically loading and unloading kernel code. They offer flexibility in managing memory usage and enable driver development without kernel recompilation.

### 5.5.1 Module Loading and Unloading

Modules are loaded using the insmod or modprobe commands. insmod loads a specific module file, while modprobe resolves dependencies and loads required modules automatically.

Modules can be unloaded with rmmod or modprobe -r. The /proc/modules file lists currently loaded modules, and lsmod provides a formatted view of loaded modules with their sizes and usage counts.

### 5.5.2 Built-in vs. Module Trade-offs

The decision to build a driver into the kernel or as a module involves several trade-offs:

- **Built-in Drivers:**Available immediately at boot, consume fixed memory, no filesystem dependency.
- **Module Drivers:**Loaded on demand, saving memory when not needed, require filesystem access to load.

For essential drivers needed during boot, built-in is preferred. For optional hardware, modules provide flexibility and reduce kernel size.

# Chapter 6: Device Drivers Development

Device drivers form the critical interface between the Linux kernel and hardware peripherals. Understanding driver architecture and development techniques is essential for embedded developers who must support custom hardware or optimize existing driver implementations.

## 6.1 Linux Driver Architecture

Linux organizes device drivers into a hierarchical model that provides consistent interfaces for driver development and device access.

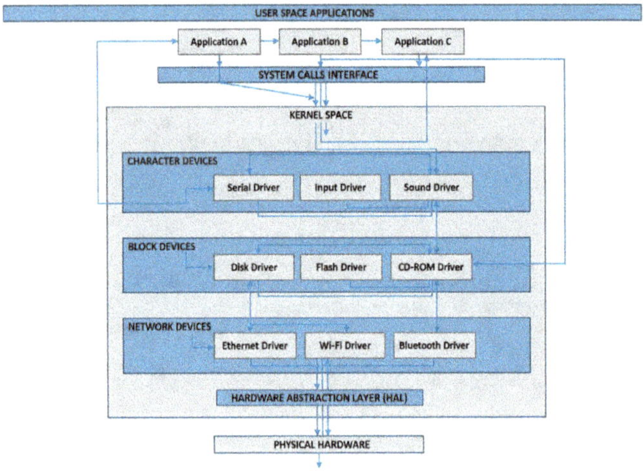


*Figure 6.1: Linux Device Driver Architecture*

### 6.1.1 The Linux Driver Model

The Linux driver model organizes devices, drivers, and buses into a unified framework. Devices represent hardware components, drivers provide the software interface to devices, and buses connect devices to the system.

This model enables automatic driver binding, power management, and consistent device naming. When a device is detected, the kernel searches for a matching driver and automatically binds them. This plug-and-play behavior simplifies system configuration and enables hot-pluggable devices.

### 6.1.2 Device Classes and Types

Linux categorizes devices into three primary types:

- **Character Devices:**Devices that provide byte-stream access, such as serial ports, sensors, and GPIO. Accessed through file operations like read() and write(). Represented by device nodes in /dev.
- **Block Devices:**Devices that provide random-access block storage, such as hard drives, flash storage, and SD cards. Accessed through the block layer with buffering and caching.
- **Network Devices:**Devices that provide network packet transmission and reception. Accessed through the socket interface rather than file operations.

## 6.2 Character Device Drivers

Character device drivers are the most common type in embedded systems, providing access to sensors, actuators, and communication interfaces.

### 6.2.1 Driver Registration

Character drivers register with the kernel using alloc_chrdev_region() to obtain a device number, cdev_init() to initialize the cdev structure, and cdev_add() to add the device to the system.

The file_operations structure defines the driver's entry points for open, release, read, write, ioctl, and other operations. This structure connects user-space system calls to driver implementations.

### 6.2.2 File Operations

The file_operations structure contains function pointers for operations that can be performed on the device:

- **open:**Called when the device is opened. Performs initialization and resource allocation. Returns a file descriptor.
- **release:**Called when the device is closed. Releases resources allocated in open.
- **read:**Reads data from the device to user space. Returns the number of bytes read.
- **write:**Writes data from user space to the device. Returns the number of bytes written.
- **ioctl:**Handles device-specific commands not covered by standard operations.
- **mmap:**Maps device memory into user space for direct access.

### 6.2.3 User Space Access

Drivers must carefully manage data transfer between kernel space and user space. The copy_to_user() and copy_from_user() functions safely transfer data, performing access verification and handling potential page faults.

Direct memory access through mmap() can improve performance for large transfers but requires careful synchronization. The remap_pfn_range() function maps physical memory pages into user space.

## 6.3 Platform Drivers

Platform drivers provide a mechanism for devices that are not discoverable through standard buses. Most embedded peripherals fall into this category, as they are integrated directly into the SoC rather than connected through PCI or USB.

### 6.3.1 Platform Device Registration

Platform devices are typically defined in the device tree, which the kernel parses to create platform_device structures. The device tree specifies hardware resources including register addresses, interrupt numbers, and clock sources.

Platform drivers register with the platform bus and are bound to matching platform devices based on compatible strings. This binding mechanism enables automatic driver loading when the corresponding hardware is present.

### 6.3.2 Resource Management

Platform drivers use the resource management framework to acquire and release hardware resources. The devm_* family of functions provides automatic resource cleanup when the driver is unbound, simplifying error handling and preventing resource leaks.

Resources include I/O memory regions (request_mem_region), interrupt lines (request_irq), DMA channels, and clocks (clk_get). Proper resource management is essential for reliable driver operation.

## 6.4 Interrupt Handling

Interrupts enable efficient handling of asynchronous hardware events. Proper interrupt handling is critical for responsive embedded systems.

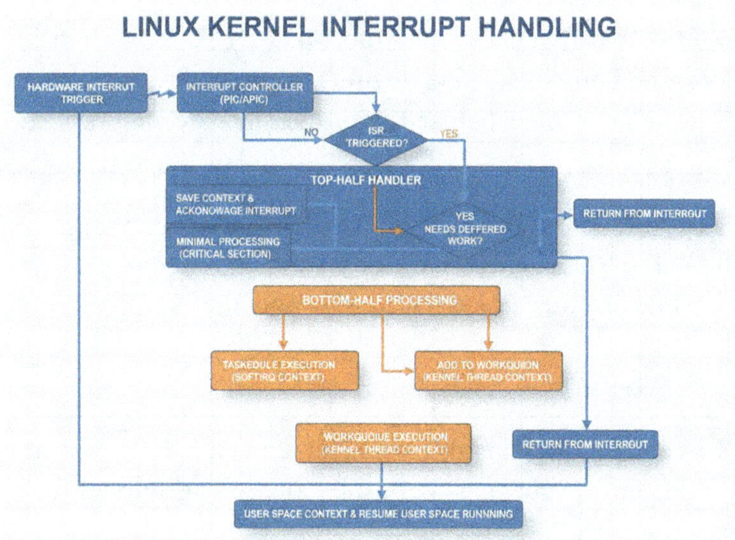


*Figure 6.2: Linux Kernel Interrupt Handling Flow*

### 6.4.1 Interrupt Registration

Drivers register interrupt handlers using request_irq() or the managed devm_request_irq(). The registration specifies the interrupt number, handler function, flags controlling interrupt behavior, and a name for identification.

The interrupt handler runs in interrupt context with restrictions on sleeping and accessing user space. It should complete quickly to avoid delaying other interrupts.

### 6.4.2 Top-Half and Bottom-Half Processing

Interrupt handlers should complete quickly to avoid delaying other interrupts. The top-half, the actual interrupt handler, performs minimal work, typically acknowledging the interrupt and scheduling deferred processing.

The bottom-half, implemented as a tasklet, workqueue, or threaded IRQ, performs the majority of processing at a lower priority. This split ensures responsive interrupt handling while allowing complex processing.

### 6.4.3 GPIO Interrupts

GPIO pins can generate interrupts on level or edge transitions. The GPIO subsystem provides gpiod_to_irq() to obtain the interrupt number for a GPIO, which can then be used with the standard interrupt registration functions.

GPIO interrupts are commonly used for button presses, sensor alerts, and external event notification. Edge-triggered interrupts detect state changes, while level-triggered interrupts respond to sustained conditions.

## 6.5 Direct Memory Access (DMA)

DMA enables peripherals to transfer data directly to or from memory without CPU involvement, significantly improving throughput for high-speed data transfers.

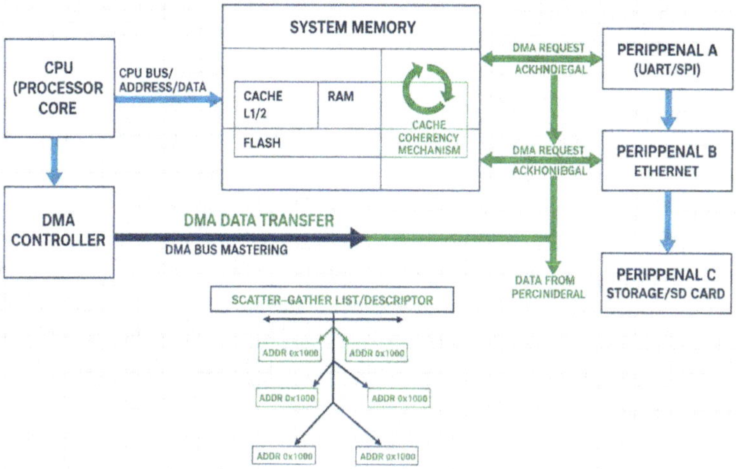


*Figure 6.3: DMA Architecture with Scatter-Gather Support*

### 6.5.1 DMA Engine Framework

The Linux DMA engine framework provides a unified interface for DMA controllers. Drivers allocate DMA channels, configure transfer parameters, and submit transfer descriptors.

The framework handles descriptor chaining, completion notification, and synchronization with CPU access to DMA buffers. This abstraction allows drivers to work with different DMA controllers through a common interface.

### 6.5.2 Cache Coherency

DMA requires careful cache management to ensure data consistency. On architectures without hardware cache coherency, drivers must explicitly flush cache lines before DMA writes and invalidate cache lines after DMA reads.

The dma_map_single() and dma_unmap_single() functions handle cache synchronization and address translation for DMA buffers. These functions ensure that CPU and DMA controller see consistent data.

## 6.6 Device Tree Bindings

Device tree bindings define the properties that describe a device to its driver. Proper binding documentation ensures consistent hardware description across platforms.

### 6.6.1 Standard Bindings

The kernel documentation includes standard bindings for common device types. These bindings specify required properties, optional properties, and their interpretation.

Using standard bindings where possible ensures compatibility with existing drivers and tooling. When a standard binding exists for a device type, it should be used rather than creating a custom binding.

### 6.6.2 Custom Bindings

Custom hardware may require custom bindings. These should be documented following the kernel's binding documentation format, specifying all properties and their values.

Custom bindings should be submitted for review to the appropriate kernel mailing list to establish them as standard bindings for future use. This contribution benefits the broader community and ensures long-term maintainability.

# Chapter 7: Root Filesystem and Storage Management

The root filesystem contains the user-space components of a Linux system: applications, libraries, configuration files, and device nodes. Designing an appropriate root filesystem for embedded systems requires careful consideration of storage constraints, reliability requirements, and update mechanisms.

## 7.1 Root Filesystem Design

The root filesystem structure follows the Filesystem Hierarchy Standard (FHS), which defines the purpose of standard directories. Embedded systems may deviate from FHS for size optimization while maintaining compatibility with standard tools and conventions.

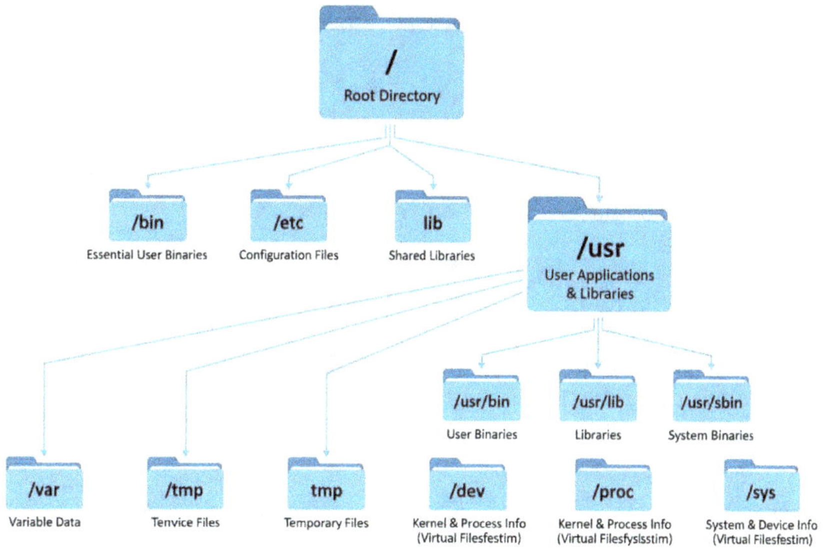


*Figure 7.1: Linux Filesystem Hierarchy Structure*

### 7.1.1 Essential Directories

Key directories in an embedded root filesystem include:

- **/bin:**Essential user commands and utilities needed for system boot and repair. These must be available even if other filesystems are not mounted.
- **/sbin:**System administration binaries, typically requiring root privileges. Includes tools for filesystem repair, network configuration, and system initialization.
- **/lib:**Essential shared libraries required by binaries in /bin and /sbin. May also contain kernel modules in /lib/modules.
- **/etc:**System-wide configuration files. Includes startup scripts, network configuration, and application settings.
- **/dev:**Device nodes providing access to hardware devices. Modern systems use devtmpfs or udev to populate this directory dynamically.
- **/proc:**Virtual filesystem exposing kernel and process information. Provides insight into system state and configuration.
- **/sys:**Virtual filesystem exposing system and device information. Enables userspace interaction with kernel objects.
- **/tmp:**Temporary files, typically mounted as a RAM-based tmpfs that is cleared on reboot.
- **/var:**Variable data including logs, caches, and spool files. Often mounted with writeable storage.

### 7.1.2 Size Optimization

Minimizing root filesystem size is often critical for embedded systems. Techniques include:

- **Smaller C Libraries:**Use musl or uClibc-ng instead of glibc for significant size reduction.
- **Binary Stripping:**Remove debug symbols and unnecessary sections from binaries.

- **Remove Locales:**Eliminate unnecessary locale data and documentation.
- **Compiler Optimization:**Use -Os optimization flag for size-optimized code generation.
- **Filesystem Compression:**Use compressed filesystems like SquashFS to reduce storage requirements.

## 7.2 Filesystem Types for Embedded Systems

Various filesystem types offer different trade-offs between performance, reliability, and features. The choice depends on the underlying storage technology and application requirements.

### 7.2.1 Read-Only Filesystems

Read-only filesystems provide reliability and corruption resistance, as the filesystem cannot be modified at runtime. This is ideal for the root filesystem in many embedded applications.

- **SquashFS:**Compressed read-only filesystem with excellent compression ratios. Widely used for live CDs and embedded systems. Supports multiple compression algorithms including gzip, LZO, and LZ4.
- **cramfs:**Older compressed read-only filesystem with limited features. Superseded by SquashFS for most applications.

### 7.2.2 Journaling Filesystems

Journaling filesystems maintain a log of pending changes, enabling quick recovery after power loss without full filesystem checks:

- **ext4:**The standard Linux filesystem with excellent performance and reliability. Supports large files and volumes, extents, and delayed allocation.
- **F2FS:**Flash-Friendly File System optimized for NAND flash storage. Reduces write amplification and improves performance on flash devices.

- **UBIFS:**Unsorted Block Image File System for raw NAND flash. Handles bad blocks and wear leveling in conjunction with the UBI layer.

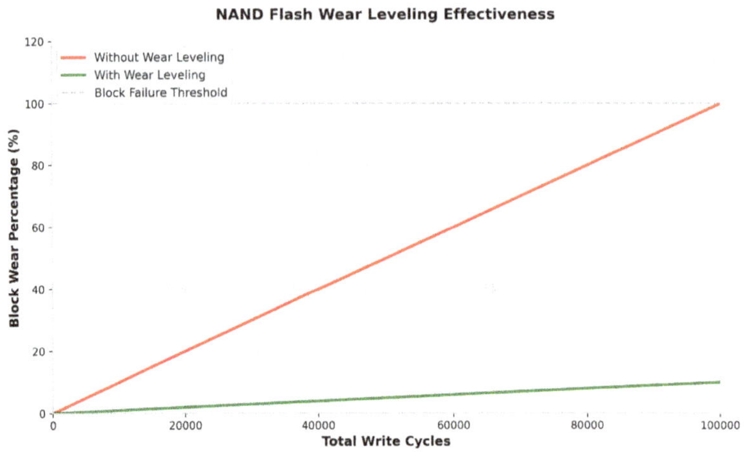


*Figure 7.2: NAND Flash Wear Leveling Effectiveness*

## 7.3 Storage Technologies

Embedded systems employ various storage technologies, each with distinct characteristics affecting filesystem design and system architecture.

*Figure 7.3: Embedded Hardware Components*

### 7.3.1 Raw NAND Flash

Raw NAND flash provides high-density, cost-effective storage but requires careful management. NAND flash has unique characteristics: blocks must be erased before writing, erase blocks are larger than write pages, blocks have limited erase cycles, and some blocks may be factory-marked as bad.

The Memory Technology Devices (MTD) subsystem provides the interface between NAND flash and higher-level software. UBI (Unsorted Block Images) provides volume management on top of MTD, handling bad blocks and wear leveling.

### 7.3.2 eMMC

eMMC (embedded MultiMediaCard) combines NAND flash with an integrated controller in a standardized package. The controller handles bad block management, wear leveling, and ECC, presenting a simple block device interface to the host.

eMMC is widely used in consumer electronics and provides a good balance of cost, capacity, and reliability. The standardized interface simplifies software design, and the integrated controller offloads complexity from the host processor.

### 7.3.3 SD and microSD Cards

SD cards provide removable storage using a similar interface to eMMC. Quality varies significantly between manufacturers and product lines. Industrial-grade SD cards offer better reliability and wider temperature ranges than consumer cards.

## 7.4 Over-the-Air Updates

OTA update capability is essential for maintaining embedded systems throughout their lifecycle. Robust update mechanisms ensure system reliability and security.

### 7.4.1 A/B Partition Schemes

A/B partitioning maintains two complete system images, with only one active at a time. Updates are written to the inactive partition, which is then activated on reboot. If the update fails, the system can fall back to the previous working version.

This approach provides atomic updates and rollback capability but requires twice the storage capacity. The additional storage cost is often justified by the improved reliability and reduced maintenance requirements.

### 7.4.2 Update Verification

Cryptographic verification ensures update integrity and authenticity. Updates should be signed by a trusted authority, with the signature verified before application. Secure boot mechanisms can extend verification to the entire boot chain.

# Chapter 8: Networking in IoT Systems

Network connectivity is the defining characteristic of IoT devices. This chapter examines the networking infrastructure, protocols, and configuration essential for embedded Linux IoT systems, from low-level interface configuration to high-level application protocols.

## 8.1 Network Interface Configuration

Linux provides a comprehensive networking stack supporting diverse interface types and configurations. Understanding network interface management is fundamental to IoT development.

### 8.1.1 Ethernet Configuration

Ethernet remains the primary wired networking technology for IoT gateways and powered devices. Network interfaces are configured through the ip command from the iproute2 package, which has superseded the older ifconfig.

Configuration includes setting IP addresses, netmasks, routes, and interface parameters. Static configuration assigns fixed addresses, while DHCP enables automatic address assignment from a server.

### 8.1.2 Wireless Networking

Wireless networking in Linux is managed through the cfg80211 and mac80211 frameworks, with device-specific drivers providing hardware support. The wpa_supplicant daemon handles authentication for WPA/WPA2 networks.

Configuration can be static or managed through network management tools. For embedded systems, lightweight tools like ConnMan or systemd-networkd are often preferred over full NetworkManager.

### 8.1.3 Network Management Tools

Several tools provide network management for embedded systems:

- **systemd-networkd:**Lightweight network configuration integrated with systemd. Suitable for servers and containers.
- **ConnMan:**Connection manager designed for embedded devices. Handles various connection types with minimal resource usage.
- **NetworkManager:**Full-featured network management with desktop integration. May be too heavyweight for minimal embedded systems.

## 8.2 TCP/IP Stack Configuration

The Linux TCP/IP stack is highly configurable, allowing optimization for specific use cases and resource constraints.

### 8.2.1 sysctl Parameters

Kernel networking parameters are controlled through sysctl, which exposes variables in /proc/sys/net/. Important parameters include buffer sizes, timeout values, congestion control algorithms, and forwarding behavior.

Tuning these parameters can significantly impact network performance and resource usage. For example, increasing socket buffer sizes improves throughput for high-bandwidth connections, while reducing them conserves memory on constrained systems.

### 8.2.2 Socket Options

Applications can configure socket behavior through setsockopt() calls. Options control keepalive behavior, buffer sizes, timeout values, and protocol-specific parameters.

Proper socket configuration is essential for reliable IoT communication, particularly over unreliable networks. TCP keepalive can detect dead connections, while appropriate timeout values prevent indefinite blocking.

## 8.3 IoT Protocol Implementation

Implementing IoT protocols requires understanding both the protocol specifications and the Linux networking APIs.

### 8.3.1 MQTT Client Implementation

MQTT clients can be implemented using libraries such as Eclipse Paho, Mosquitto, or custom implementations. Key considerations include connection management with automatic reconnection, publish/subscribe handling, quality of service selection, and proper handling of the last will and testament.

For resource-constrained devices, lightweight implementations like MQTT-C or embedded Mosquitto are preferred. These implementations minimize memory usage while providing essential MQTT functionality.

### 8.3.2 CoAP Implementation

CoAP implementations include libcoap, microcoap, and custom solutions. CoAP's RESTful model maps well to HTTP concepts, making it accessible to developers familiar with web services.

Implementation considerations include message deduplication, block-wise transfers for large payloads, and observation subscriptions for event notification.

### 8.3.3 HTTP/REST APIs

HTTP client functionality is provided by libraries such as libcurl, which supports a wide range of protocols and features. For minimal systems, lighter alternatives like http-client or custom implementations using raw sockets may be appropriate.

## 8.4 Network Security

Network security is critical for IoT devices, which often operate in untrusted environments and may have physical accessibility to attackers.

### 8.4.1 TLS/SSL Implementation

Transport Layer Security (TLS) provides encrypted, authenticated communication. OpenSSL is the standard TLS library but may be too large for constrained devices.

Alternatives include mbed TLS (formerly PolarSSL), wolfSSL, and BearSSL, which offer smaller footprints suitable for embedded systems. Certificate management, including validation and renewal, must be carefully designed.

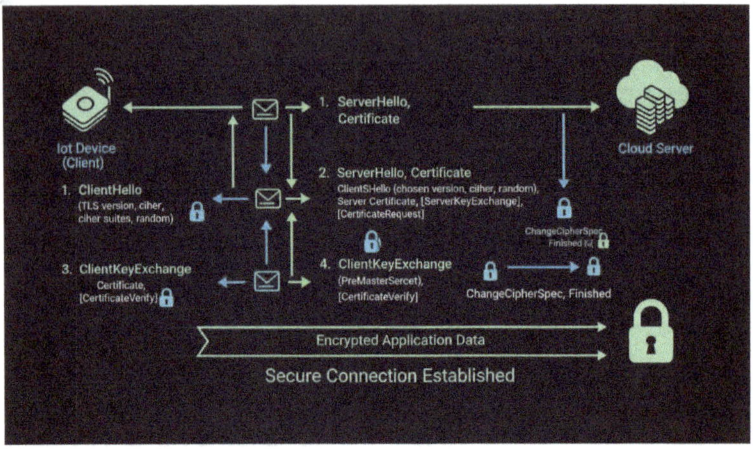


*Figure 8.1: TLS Handshake Process for IoT Device Authentication*

### 8.4.2 Firewall and Access Control

Linux provides netfilter/iptables and the newer nftables for packet filtering and network address translation. Minimal embedded systems should configure firewalls to allow only necessary traffic, reducing the attack surface.

Default-deny policies with explicit rules for required connections provide strong security. Only ports and protocols required for application functionality should be opened.

## 8.5 Network Debugging

Debugging network issues in embedded systems requires familiarity with Linux networking tools and techniques.

### 8.5.1 Packet Capture and Analysis

tcpdump provides command-line packet capture, which can be analyzed with Wireshark on a development host. Capturing on the device itself may be necessary when issues cannot be reproduced in other environments.

### 8.5.2 Network Diagnostics

Standard diagnostic tools including ping, traceroute, netstat, and ss help identify connectivity and routing issues. The ss command from iproute2 provides more detailed socket information than the older netstat.

# Chapter 9: Security for IoT Devices

Security is a paramount concern for IoT systems, where compromised devices can have serious real-world consequences. This chapter examines security threats facing IoT devices and presents comprehensive strategies for building secure embedded Linux systems.

## 9.1 IoT Security Threats

IoT devices face a diverse threat landscape due to their deployment characteristics: often physically accessible, continuously connected, and resource-constrained.

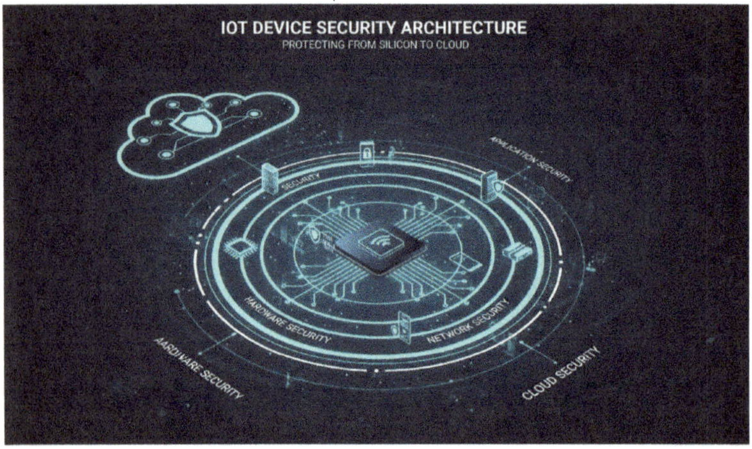


*Figure 9.1: IoT Device Security Architecture - Multi-Layer Protection*

### 9.1.1 Physical Attacks

Physical access enables attacks including firmware extraction from flash chips, JTAG debugging interface exploitation, side-channel analysis of power consumption or electromagnetic emissions, and bus sniffing or injection.

Devices deployed in unsecured locations must implement countermeasures against physical tampering. These include secure boot to prevent unauthorized firmware execution, encrypted storage to protect sensitive data, and tamper detection mechanisms.

### 9.1.2 Network Attacks

Network-connected devices are exposed to attacks including man-in-the-middle interception, denial of service flooding, exploitation of protocol vulnerabilities, and credential theft or brute force attacks.

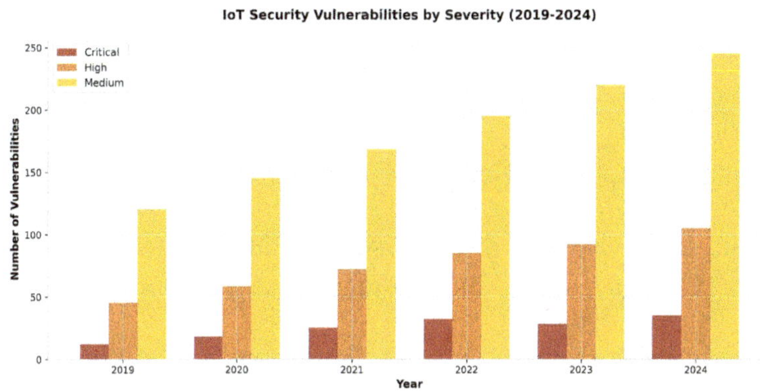


*Figure 9.2: IoT Security Vulnerabilities by Severity (2019-2024)*

## 9.2 Secure Boot

Secure boot establishes a chain of trust from hardware reset through operating system loading, ensuring only authentic, unmodified software executes.

### 9.2.1 Chain of Trust

The secure boot chain begins with a hardware root of trust, typically ROM code that verifies the bootloader. The verified bootloader then verifies the kernel, which may verify the initramfs or root filesystem.

Each stage cryptographically verifies the next before execution. Breaks in this chain allow attackers to inject malicious code. The entire chain must be protected for secure boot to be effective.

### 9.2.2 Implementation with U-Boot

U-Boot supports secure boot through FIT (Flattened Image Tree) images containing cryptographic signatures. The mkimage tool creates signed images, and U-Boot verifies signatures using embedded public keys.

### 9.2.3 Key Management

Secure boot requires careful key management. Private keys used for signing must be protected in hardware security modules or secure offline storage. Public keys embedded in devices for verification must be immutable.

## 9.3 Access Control and Authentication

Controlling access to device resources and authenticating users and services prevents unauthorized operations.

### 9.3.1 Linux Access Control

Linux implements discretionary access control (DAC) through traditional Unix permissions. Files and processes have owner, group, and world permissions controlling read, write, and execute access.

For IoT devices, the principle of least privilege should be applied: processes run with minimal necessary permissions, and sensitive resources are protected appropriately.

### 9.3.2 Mandatory Access Control

Mandatory access control (MAC) systems like SELinux and AppArmor provide additional security beyond DAC. MAC policies define what actions processes can perform, regardless of traditional ownership.

### 9.3.3 Authentication Mechanisms

Device authentication to cloud services typically uses X.509 certificates or pre-shared keys. Certificate-based authentication provides stronger security but requires certificate management infrastructure.

## 9.4 Encryption

Encryption protects data confidentiality both in transit and at rest, preventing unauthorized access to sensitive information.

### 9.4.1 Data in Transit

Network communication should be encrypted using TLS for TCP-based protocols or DTLS for UDP-based protocols. TLS 1.3 provides improved security and performance compared to earlier versions.

### 9.4.2 Data at Rest

Sensitive data stored on the device requires encryption to protect against physical access attacks. Full-disk encryption using dm-crypt protects the entire filesystem.

## 9.5 Security Hardening

Security hardening reduces the attack surface by removing unnecessary components and configuring the system securely.

### 9.5.1 Minimization

Each component in the system is a potential vulnerability. Removing unnecessary services, libraries, and kernel features reduces the attack surface.

### 9.5.2 Compiler Hardening

Compiler flags can generate more secure binaries. Position-independent executables (PIE) enable address space layout randomization (ASLR). Stack canaries detect stack buffer overflows.

### 9.5.3 Runtime Protections

Linux provides runtime protections including ASLR, which randomizes memory addresses to thwart exploits; non-executable stacks and heaps preventing code execution from data pages; and ptrace restrictions preventing process debugging.

## 9.6 Security Monitoring and Updates

Ongoing security monitoring and timely updates are essential for maintaining system security throughout the device lifecycle.

### 9.6.1 Logging and Monitoring

Security-relevant events should be logged for analysis and audit. The systemd journal or syslog daemons collect log messages. Remote logging to centralized servers protects logs from tampering.

### 9.6.2 Vulnerability Management

A process for tracking and responding to security vulnerabilities is essential. This includes monitoring security advisories for Linux, libraries, and applications; assessing vulnerability impact on the specific system configuration; and developing and deploying patches in a timely manner.

### 9.6.3 Secure Update Mechanisms

OTA updates must themselves be secure to prevent installation of malicious firmware. Updates should be cryptographically signed, with verification before installation. The update mechanism should handle interrupted updates gracefully and support rollback to known-good versions.

# Chapter 10: Cloud Integration and Protocols

Cloud integration transforms standalone IoT devices into components of larger distributed systems. This chapter examines the architecture, protocols, and implementation strategies for connecting embedded Linux devices to cloud platforms.

## 10.1 Cloud Architecture for IoT

IoT cloud architectures must handle massive scale, diverse device types, and varying data patterns while providing reliability, security, and real-time capabilities.

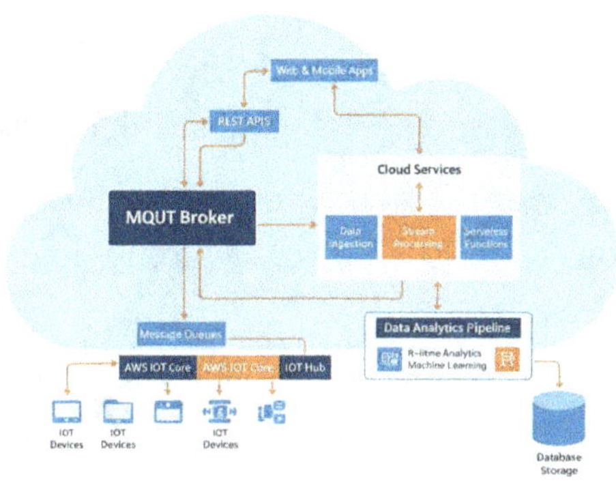


*Figure 10.1: Cloud Integration Architecture for IoT Systems*

### 10.1.1 Cloud Platform Components

IoT cloud platforms typically provide several core services:

- **Device Provisioning and Management:**Registration, authentication, and lifecycle management of connected devices.
- **Message Ingestion:**Scalable message queues and brokers handling high-volume data ingestion from devices.

- **Data Storage:**Time-series databases for sensor data, document stores for device state, and blob storage for large objects.
- **Stream Processing:**Real-time analysis and transformation of incoming data streams.
- **Rule Engines:**Event-driven processing triggering actions based on data patterns.
- **Analytics and Machine Learning:**Historical analysis, anomaly detection, and predictive modeling.
- **Visualization:**Dashboards and reporting interfaces for monitoring and insights.

### 10.1.2 Major Cloud Platforms

Several cloud providers offer comprehensive IoT platforms:

- **AWS IoT Core:**Managed cloud service enabling secure device connectivity and messaging. Integrates with extensive AWS services.
- **Azure IoT Hub:**Central message hub for bidirectional communication with IoT devices. Strong integration with Azure analytics services.
- **Google Cloud IoT Core:**Fully managed service for connecting and managing devices with integration to Google Cloud data services.
- **IBM Watson IoT Platform:**Enterprise-focused platform with strong device management and analytics capabilities.

## 10.2 MQTT in Production

MQTT is the dominant protocol for IoT messaging. Production deployments require careful attention to broker selection, topic design, and client implementation.

### 10.2.1 MQTT Broker Selection

Several MQTT broker implementations are suitable for production use:

- **Eclipse Mosquitto:**Lightweight open-source broker suitable for edge deployment and smaller cloud installations.
- **EMQ X:**High-performance broker supporting millions of concurrent connections. Enterprise features include clustering and monitoring.
- **HiveMQ:**Enterprise broker with strong support for MQTT 5.0 and cloud-native deployment options.
- **VerneMQ:**Distributed broker designed for high availability and horizontal scalability.

### 10.2.2 Topic Namespace Design

Well-designed topic namespaces enable clean separation of concerns and efficient message routing. Common patterns include hierarchical structures with device ID, location, and sensor type.

### 10.2.3 Quality of Service Selection

MQTT provides three QoS levels with different delivery guarantees. QoS 0 provides at-most-once delivery with minimal overhead. QoS 1 provides at-least-once delivery with acknowledgment. QoS 2 provides exactly-once delivery with higher overhead, rarely needed in practice.

## 10.3 REST API Integration

REST APIs provide a familiar, well-supported interface for IoT device communication and management.

### 10.3.1 API Design for IoT

REST APIs for IoT should follow standard HTTP semantics while accommodating device constraints. Resource-oriented URLs identify devices, sensors, and data. Standard HTTP methods (GET, POST, PUT, DELETE) manipulate resources.

### 10.3.2 Authentication and Authorization

API authentication commonly uses API keys, OAuth 2.0 tokens, or mutual TLS. API keys are simple but less secure. OAuth 2.0 provides token-based authentication with scope-based authorization. Mutual TLS provides strong authentication through client certificates.

### 10.3.3 Rate Limiting and Throttling

Cloud APIs typically implement rate limiting to prevent abuse and ensure fair resource sharing. Devices must handle rate limit responses (HTTP 429) with appropriate backoff and retry strategies.

## 10.4 Edge Computing

Edge computing processes data near its source, reducing latency, bandwidth, and cloud dependency.

### 10.4.1 Edge Gateway Architecture

Edge gateways aggregate data from multiple sensors, perform local processing, and communicate with the cloud. Gateway software stacks include protocol translation, local data buffering, rule engines, and device management agents.

### 10.4.2 Local Analytics

Edge analytics can filter, aggregate, and transform data before cloud transmission. This reduces bandwidth costs and enables real-time response. Lightweight machine learning inference at the edge supports applications like anomaly detection.

### 10.4.3 Offline Operation

Robust IoT systems must handle intermittent connectivity gracefully. Local data buffering stores messages during outages for later transmission. Local rule engines enable autonomous operation when cloud connectivity is unavailable.

## 10.5 Device Management

Managing fleets of IoT devices requires comprehensive device management capabilities.

### 10.5.1 Device Lifecycle Management

Device lifecycle management encompasses provisioning, configuration, monitoring, and retirement. Provisioning establishes device identity and credentials. Configuration management applies settings and parameters. Monitoring tracks device health and connectivity.

### 10.5.2 Remote Diagnostics

Remote diagnostics enable troubleshooting without physical device access. Capabilities include remote log access, command execution for debugging, metrics collection for performance analysis, and configuration inspection.

### 10.5.3 Bulk Operations

Managing large device fleets requires bulk operation capabilities. Bulk configuration updates apply settings across device groups. Bulk firmware updates deploy new software versions. Job tracking monitors progress and results of bulk operations.

# Chapter 11: Case Studies and Applications

This chapter presents real-world case studies illustrating the design decisions, implementation strategies, and lessons learned from deploying embedded Linux IoT systems across various industry verticals.

## 11.1 Industrial Predictive Maintenance System

A manufacturing company deployed a predictive maintenance system to monitor critical machinery and predict failures before they occur, reducing downtime and maintenance costs.

### 11.1.1 System Architecture

The system consists of vibration and temperature sensors mounted on motors, pumps, and gearboxes. Sensor nodes based on ARM Cortex-M4 microcontrollers sample data at high frequency and perform local FFT analysis.

Gateway devices running embedded Linux aggregate data from multiple sensors and perform edge analytics. The cloud platform stores historical data and runs machine learning models for failure prediction.

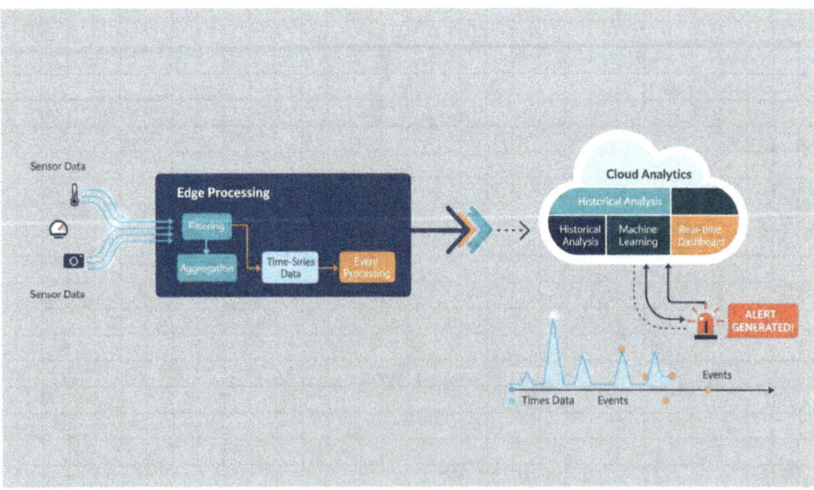


*Figure 11.1: Real-Time Data Processing Pipeline for Industrial IoT*

### 11.1.2 Technical Implementation

The gateway runs a custom Yocto-based Linux distribution optimized for industrial environments. Key components include:

- **Kernel Configuration:**Real-time kernel with PREEMPT_RT patch for consistent sensor sampling timing.
- **Protocol Stack:**Modbus RTU for sensor communication, MQTT for cloud connectivity.
- **Edge Analytics:**Python-based analysis pipeline using NumPy for signal processing.
- **Local Storage:**SQLite database for buffering data during network outages.
- **Security:**Hardware secure element for device authentication, TLS 1.3 for cloud communication.

### 11.1.3 Results and Lessons

The system achieved 95% accuracy in predicting bearing failures 48 hours in advance. Key lessons included the importance of robust offline operation, the value of edge analytics in reducing cloud costs, and the necessity of industrial-grade hardware.

## 11.2 Smart Agriculture Monitoring

A large agricultural operation deployed a comprehensive monitoring system for irrigation management, soil health tracking, and crop optimization across thousands of acres.

### 11.2.1 System Requirements

The system needed to cover extensive areas with limited cellular coverage, operate on battery power for entire growing seasons, withstand outdoor environmental conditions, and provide actionable insights to farm managers.

### 11.2.2 Network Architecture

The deployment uses a multi-tier network architecture. Soil moisture sensors and weather stations communicate via LoRaWAN to gateway devices positioned throughout the fields. LoRaWAN provides excellent range and penetration while consuming minimal power.

### 11.2.3 Power Optimization

Power optimization was critical for battery-operated sensors. Strategies included deep sleep between measurements with wake intervals of 15 minutes, aggressive power management disabling all unused peripherals, efficient data transmission using binary CBOR encoding, and adaptive sampling reducing frequency during stable conditions.

### 11.2.4 Outcomes

The system reduced water consumption by 30% through precision irrigation while maintaining crop yields. Frost alerts enabled protective action that prevented significant crop losses.

## 11.3 Connected Healthcare Devices

A medical device manufacturer developed a connected platform for remote patient monitoring, enabling healthcare providers to track patient health outside clinical settings.

### 11.3.1 Regulatory Considerations

Medical devices face stringent regulatory requirements including FDA clearance in the United States and CE marking in Europe. The Linux-based components required extensive documentation, risk analysis, and testing to demonstrate safety and effectiveness.

### 11.3.2 Security Architecture

The security architecture implemented multiple protective layers. Hardware secure elements stored device certificates and encryption keys.

Secure boot verified all software before execution. Full-disk encryption protected patient data at rest.

### 11.3.3 Data Privacy

HIPAA compliance required comprehensive data privacy measures. Data minimization collected only necessary information. Encryption protected data throughout its lifecycle. Access controls limited data access to authorized healthcare providers.

## 11.4 Smart Building Energy Management

A commercial real estate company deployed an energy management system across multiple office buildings to reduce energy consumption and operating costs.

### 11.4.1 Integration Challenges

The system needed to integrate with existing building systems including HVAC controllers from multiple vendors, lighting systems with proprietary protocols, occupancy sensors and access control systems, and utility meters with various interfaces.

### 11.4.2 Control Strategies

The system implemented multiple control strategies for energy optimization. Occupancy-based HVAC adjustment reduced heating and cooling in unoccupied spaces. Daylight harvesting adjusted artificial lighting based on natural light levels.

### 11.4.3 Economic Impact

The system achieved 25% reduction in energy costs across the building portfolio. Peak demand reduction lowered demand charges from utilities. Tenant satisfaction improved through better temperature control and lighting quality.

# Chapter 12: Future Trends and Conclusion

The field of embedded Linux IoT systems continues to evolve rapidly, driven by technological advances, changing market demands, and emerging applications. This chapter explores trends that will shape the future of this domain and provides concluding thoughts for practitioners.

## 12.1 Emerging Hardware Architectures

Hardware evolution continues to expand the capabilities and efficiency of embedded systems.

### 12.1.1 RISC-V Adoption

RISC-V, an open instruction set architecture, is gaining significant traction in embedded applications. Its open nature eliminates licensing fees and enables customization for specific applications. Linux support for RISC-V is maturing rapidly, with mainline kernel support and growing ecosystem support.

### 12.1.2 AI Acceleration at the Edge

Neural network accelerators are becoming common in embedded processors, enabling on-device machine learning inference. These accelerators dramatically improve performance and efficiency for workloads like image recognition, voice processing, and anomaly detection.

### 12.1.3 Advanced Process Nodes

Semiconductor process advances enable more powerful processors with lower power consumption. 5nm and smaller processes pack more transistors into the same die area while reducing power.

## 12.2 Software Evolution

Software platforms and development practices continue to evolve to meet IoT requirements.

### 12.2.1 Containerization for IoT

Container technologies like Docker and containerd are adapting for embedded deployment. Containers provide application isolation, simplified deployment, and consistent runtime environments.

### 12.2.2 WebAssembly at the Edge

WebAssembly (Wasm) provides a portable, sandboxed execution environment with near-native performance. Wasm modules can run on diverse platforms without modification, enabling write-once, deploy-anywhere applications.

### 12.2.3 Declarative Configuration

Infrastructure-as-code practices are extending to device configuration. Tools like Ansible, Puppet, and specialized IoT platforms enable declarative device configuration, where the desired state is specified and the system automatically converges to that state.

## 12.3 Connectivity Evolution

Network connectivity options continue to expand, offering new capabilities for IoT deployments.

### 12.3.1 5G and Private Networks

5G networks offer higher bandwidth, lower latency, and support for massive device density. Private 5G networks provide dedicated spectrum for industrial and enterprise deployments, offering guaranteed performance and enhanced security.

### 12.3.2 Satellite IoT

Satellite connectivity extends IoT to remote areas without terrestrial network coverage. Low Earth Orbit (LEO) satellite constellations offer lower latency and cost compared to traditional geostationary satellites.

### 12.3.3 Mesh and Ad-Hoc Networks

Mesh networking protocols enable device-to-device communication without infrastructure, extending range and improving reliability. Thread and Zigbee continue to evolve for home and building automation.

## 12.4 Security Evolution

Security remains a critical concern as IoT deployments expand and threats evolve.

### 12.4.1 Post-Quantum Cryptography

Quantum computers threaten current public-key cryptography algorithms. Post-quantum cryptographic algorithms, resistant to quantum attacks, are being standardized. IoT devices with long deployment lifetimes must plan for post-quantum migration.

### 12.4.2 Zero Trust Architecture

Zero trust security models assume no implicit trust based on network location. Every access request is authenticated and authorized, regardless of source. Implementing zero trust in IoT requires strong device identity and fine-grained access controls.

### 12.4.3 Automated Security Response

Security orchestration and automated response (SOAR) extends to IoT deployments. Automated systems detect anomalies, isolate compromised devices, and deploy countermeasures without human intervention.

## 12.5 Conclusion

Embedded Linux IoT systems represent a convergence of technologies that is transforming industries and enabling new capabilities. This book has provided comprehensive coverage of the knowledge and skills required to design, develop, and deploy these systems.

Key principles for successful IoT development include:

- **Start with Requirements:**Clearly define functional, performance, security, and environmental requirements before beginning design.
- **Security by Design:**Integrate security considerations from the beginning rather than adding them as an afterthought.
- **Plan for the Lifecycle:**Consider the entire product lifecycle from manufacturing through end-of-life, including updates and maintenance.
- **Optimize Appropriately:**Focus optimization efforts on areas that matter for the specific application and constraints.
- **Test Thoroughly:**Comprehensive testing, including edge cases and failure modes, is essential for reliable systems.
- **Embrace Open Source:**Leverage the extensive open-source ecosystem while contributing back when possible.

The field continues to evolve, with new hardware capabilities, software technologies, and connectivity options emerging regularly. Successful practitioners maintain current knowledge while building strong foundations in the underlying principles that remain constant.

The future of embedded Linux IoT systems is bright, with expanding applications across every industry sector. From smart cities to precision agriculture, from healthcare to industrial automation, these technologies are enabling a more connected, efficient, and intelligent world.

# References

This section provides a comprehensive list of references, including books, academic papers, technical documentation, and online resources used throughout this book.

## Books


**[1]**Love, R. (2010). Linux Kernel Development (3rd ed.). Addison-Wesley Professional.

**[2]**Corbet, J., Rubini, A., & Kroah-Hartman, G. (2005). Linux Device Drivers (3rd ed.). O'Reilly Media.

**[3]**Yaghmour, K. (2008). Building Embedded Linux Systems (2nd ed.). O'Reilly Media.

**[4]**Hallinan, C. (2010). Embedded Linux Primer: A Practical Real-World Approach (2nd ed.). Prentice Hall.

**[5]**Simmonds, C. (2015). Mastering Embedded Linux Programming. Packt Publishing.

**[6]**McCool, M., Reinders, J., & Robison, A. (2012). Structured Parallel Programming: Patterns for Efficient Computation. Morgan Kaufmann.

**[7]**Stevens, W. R. (1994). TCP/IP Illustrated, Volume 1: The Protocols. Addison-Wesley Professional.

**[8]**Schneier, B. (2015). Applied Cryptography: Protocols, Algorithms and Source Code in C (20th Anniversary ed.). Wiley.

**[9]**Newman, C. (2021). Building Microservices: Designing Fine-Grained Systems (2nd ed.). O'Reilly Media.

**[10]**Kleppmann, M. (2017). Designing Data-Intensive Applications: The Big Ideas Behind Reliable, Scalable, and Maintainable Systems. O'Reilly Media.


## Technical Documentation


**[11]**Linux Kernel Documentation. The Linux Kernel Archives. https://www.kernel.org/doc/html/latest/

**[12]**U-Boot Documentation. DENX Software Engineering. https://u-boot.readthedocs.io/

**[13]**Yocto Project Documentation. Linux Foundation. https://docs.yoctoproject.org/

**[14]**Buildroot User Manual. Buildroot Association. https://buildroot.org/downloads/manual/manual.html

**[15]**Device Tree Specification. DeviceTree.org. https://www.devicetree.org/specifications/

**[16]**ARM Architecture Reference Manual. ARM Limited. https://developer.arm.com/documentation

**[17]**MQTT Version 5.0 Specification. OASIS Open. https://docs.oasis-open.org/mqtt/mqtt/v5.0/mqtt-v5.0.html

**[18]**CoAP Protocol Specification. RFC 7252. IETF. https://tools.ietf.org/html/rfc7252

**[19]**TLS 1.3 Specification. RFC 8446. IETF. https://tools.ietf.org/html/rfc8446

**[20]**OpenSSL Documentation. OpenSSL Software Foundation. https://www.openssl.org/docs/

## Academic Papers

**[21]**Stankovic, J. A. (2014). Research Directions for the Internet of Things. IEEE Internet of Things Journal, 1(1), 3-9.

**[22]**Al-Fuqaha, A., Guizani, M., Mohammadi, M., Aledhari, M., & Ayyash, M. (2015). Internet of Things: A Survey on Enabling Technologies, Protocols, and Applications. IEEE Communications Surveys & Tutorials, 17(4), 2347-2376.

**[23]**Sicari, S., Rizzardi, A., Grieco, L. A., & Coen-Porisini, A. (2015). Security, Privacy and Trust in Internet of Things: The Road Ahead. Computer Networks, 76, 146-164.

**[24]**Zanella, A., Bui, N., Castellani, A., Vangelista, L., & Zorzi, M. (2014). Internet of Things for Smart Cities. IEEE Internet of Things Journal, 1(1), 22-32.

**[25]**Bormann, C., Ersue, M., & Keranen, A. (2014). Terminology for Constrained-Node Networks. RFC 7228. IETF.

**[26]**Shelby, Z., Hartke, K., & Bormann, C. (2014). The Constrained Application Protocol (CoAP). RFC 7252. IETF.

**[27]**Mell, P., & Grance, T. (2011). The NIST Definition of Cloud Computing. NIST Special Publication 800-145.

**[28]**Stallings, W. (2017). Foundations of Modern Networking: SDN, NFV, QoE, IoT, and Cloud. Addison-Wesley Professional.

## Industry Standards

**[29]**ISO/IEC 30141:2018. Internet of Things (IoT) - Reference Architecture. International Organization for Standardization.

**[30]**IEC 62443: Industrial Communication Networks - Network and System Security. International Electrotechnical Commission.

**[31]**NIST Cybersecurity Framework. National Institute of Standards and Technology. https://www.nist.gov/cyberframework

**[32]**ETSI EN 303 645: Cyber Security for Consumer Internet of Things. European Telecommunications Standards Institute.

**[33]**OCF Specification. Open Connectivity Foundation. https://openconnectivity.org/developer/specifications/

**[34]**Matter Specification. Connectivity Standards Alliance. https://csa-iot.org/all-solutions/matter/

## Online Resources

**[35]**Embedded Linux Wiki. https://elinux.org/

**[36]**Linux Foundation. https://www.linuxfoundation.org/

**[37]**ARM Developer Resources. https://developer.arm.com/

**[38]**Eclipse IoT. https://iot.eclipse.org/

**[39]**OWASP IoT Security Project. https://owasp.org/www-project-internet-of-things/

**[40]**IoT Security Foundation. https://www.iotsecurityfoundation.org/

**[41]**AWS IoT Documentation. https://docs.aws.amazon.com/iot/

**[42]**Azure IoT Documentation. https://docs.microsoft.com/en-us/azure/iot-hub/
**[43]**Google Cloud IoT Documentation. https://cloud.google.com/iot/docs
**[44]**LWN.net - Linux Weekly News. https://lwn.net/
**[45]**Linux Kernel Mailing List. https://lkml.org/

## Conference Proceedings

**[46]**Embedded Linux Conference. Linux Foundation. Annual conference proceedings.
**[47]**IoT World. Informa Tech. Annual conference proceedings.
**[48]**ACM Conference on Embedded Networked Sensor Systems (SenSys).
**[49]**IEEE International Conference on Internet of Things (iThings).
**[50]**USENIX Security Symposium.

Additional references and resources are available through the book's companion website and online community forums. The rapidly evolving nature of IoT technology means that practitioners should regularly consult current documentation and community resources for the latest best practices and security recommendations.

# Author's Biography

***Pr Abdellatif Rahmoun.*** *I am presently teaching as a full professor in computer engineering at the Higher school of Computer science (www.ESI-SBA.dz); Algeria. In the past 30 years; I have been Intensively involved in research that focus on Artificial Intelligence. I am also actively involved as editorial board member and reviewer in several international journals (iasted, iaeng, theijet, ijopcam, Elsevier, Wiley,….).* *ORCID ID : 0000-0002-8227-3322*

***Dr. Hamdane Bensenane***

*PhD in computer sciences. Assistant professor at the higher school of Computer sciences (ESI-SBA, Algeria) since 2016.*
*I am also intensively involved in research in domain areas in Artificial intelligence particularly Machine learning, embedded systems, IoT and big data.*
*https://www.esi-sba.dz/fr/index.php/personnel/bensenane-hamdan/*

www.ingramcontent.com/pod-product-compliance
Lightning Source LLC
LaVergne TN
LVHW022308200926
848481LV00004B/1245